I0095818

This book has a vital "back-to-basics" message for our time. One of Lou Priolo's goals for this book is to assist those seeking counsel as well as those who refer people to counselors to evaluate if counseling is truly biblical. This is crucial as many Christians have become enamored with the term biblical counseling but are either unaware or unconcerned with the history and foundations of true biblical counseling. The twelve presuppositions indeed take the reader back to the basics of historical biblical counseling.

– **John Babler, PhD, Chairman and Professor, Department of Biblical Counseling, Mid-America Baptist Theological Seminary, Cordova, TN; Fellow and trustee, Association of Certified Biblical Counselors**

In light of his lifelong experience in biblical counseling and long-standing relationship with Jay Adams, Lou Priolo works through twelve important presuppositions of historic biblical counseling. Using Adams's work as his backdrop for thinking, Lou seeks to anchor the biblical counselor's practice in a nuanced theology by further developing the lens through which the counselor sees the connection between God, the person, and the circumstance. As a professor of biblical counseling, I know this resource is a great addition to helping students get a well-balanced view of biblical counseling.

– **Kevin Carson, DMin, Pastor of Sonrise Baptist Church, Ozark, MO, and Professor of Biblical Counseling at Baptist Bible College and Theological Seminary, Springfield, MO**

Lou Priolo has written a very insightful book on what historical biblical counselors really believe. The twelve presuppositions are clear, easy to understand, and completely backed by Scripture. Many Christian counselors today integrate psychology theory with the Scriptures and, thus, call themselves biblical counselors; they would benefit greatly from reading this book.

– **Martha Peace, BSN, MABC, Author, *The Excellent Wife***

Wise markers by which to measure our thinking and practice of biblical counseling. Priolo reminds us that our practice is connected to our thinking and our methods are driven by our philosophy. He offers healthy parameters anchored in Scripture to ensure that Christian counselors counsel as distinctively Christian.

– T. Dale Johnson Jr., PhD, President, Association of Certified Biblical Counselors

PRESUPPOSITIONS
OF
BIBLICAL
COUNSELING

PRESUPPOSITIONS OF BIBLICAL COUNSELING

WHAT HISTORICAL BIBLICAL COUNSELORS REALLY BELIEVE

LOU PRIOLO

GRACE & TRUTH
BOOKS

Presuppositions of Biblical Counseling
Copyright © 2023 by Louis Paul Priolo
All Rights Reserved.

This book has been reconstructed from a series of articles first published in the *Journal of Modern Ministry* (a publication of Timeless Texts), 2004–2007. Those articles have been revised and otherwise amended for this publication. Used by permission.

Published by:
Grace & Truth Books
815 Exchange Ave., Ste. 101
Conway, AR 72032
www.graceandtruthbooks.com
918.245.1500

Unless otherwise marked, Scripture quotations are taken from the (NASB®) New American Standard Bible®, Copyright © 1960, 1971, 1977, 1995 by The Lockman Foundation. Used by permission. All rights reserved. lockman.org.

Scripture quotations marked ESV are from the ESV® Bible (The Holy Bible, English Standard Version®), copyright © 2001 by Crossway, a publishing ministry of Good News Publishers. Used by permission. All rights reserved. The ESV text may not be quoted in any publication made available to the public by a Creative Commons license. The ESV may not be translated in whole or in part into any other language.

Scripture quotations marked PHILLIPS are from *The New Testament in Modern English* by J.B Phillips copyright © 1960, 1972 J. B. Phillips. Administered by The Archbishops' Council of the Church of England. Used by Permission.

Scripture marked NKJV taken from the New King James Version®. Copyright © 1982 by Thomas Nelson. Used by permission. All rights reserved.

Emphasis in Scripture quotations are the author's.

Cover design by Scott Schaller Designs
Printed in the United States of America
ISBN: 978-1-960297-09-9

Contents

Author's Note

Allow me to give you a bit of my personal testimony before we look at the presuppositions. I have been counseling full-time for over thirty-five years. I have probably logged at least thirty-two thousand hours of counseling. Interestingly, I never really wanted to be a counselor—especially a full-time counselor! But years ago, many of my Bible college friends and professors began expressing that they believed the Lord had given me some kind of "counseling gift." They said, "Lou, you should go to graduate school to put some polish on this gift or ability the Lord has given you."

"How boring," I thought. "Helping people solve their personal difficulties up to this point has been fun, but sitting behind a desk, listening to problems day after day, is not at all what I want to do with the rest of my life."

On the other hand, so many people were encouraging me to go to graduate school (to obtain a counseling degree) that I figured the Lord wanted me to go. "After all," I reasoned, "'by the mouth of two or three witnesses the matter shall be established' (Deut. 19:15), and I've got more people than that urging me to do this. Perhaps I'll be able to use what I learn in some other pastoral kind of ministry. But I still don't want to be 'a counselor.'"

So off I went, thinking that the Christian university I chose would be biblically oriented. Boy, was I in for a rude awakening! Suffice it to say that this particular graduate school was not at all what I thought it would be. Yet God, in his gracious providence, used this experience to totally change the course of my life.

After the initial shock of finding myself in the midst of an integrationist counseling program wore off, I began diving deeply into my psychological studies. Day after day, week after week, as I began imbibing those ungodly philosophies (theologies, really) of man and how he is supposed to change, I began to realize how poverty-stricken and dangerous these "state of the art" humanistic theories and methods of counseling really are. I soon realized that my little bit of Bible knowledge was far superior to the "worldly wisdom" in the theories I was being taught. Then one day, it dawned on me: "This stuff can't compete with the Scriptures. There is certainly *no competition* to a biblical counseling approach. I can do this, and by God's grace, I can do it much better than those who depend on methods and theories of change designed to leave God out of the process."

From that moment on, I was committed to (and excited about) learning how to become a biblical counselor. Again, it was the realization that nothing could compete with the Scriptures (the gospel of Christ) when it comes to changing people's lives that the Holy Spirit used to motivate me (to *call* me, if you please) to the ministry of counseling.

To pastors and counselors reading this book and wondering if the kind of counseling you do is firmly rooted in Scripture, I pray that the pages ahead will be a blessing. May they not only help you evaluate the methods, means, and motives you use in your attempt to help others but also help you move closer to the goal of using your gifts and abilities for the glory of God and the benefit of those to whom you minister.

INTRODUCTION

THE BIBLICAL COUNSELING movement is exploding all around the globe. More and more people want to identify with this movement. The term *biblical counseling* has become so popular and incorporates such a broad spectrum of counselors who profess to use the Scriptures in their counseling that many are confused as to what a biblical counselor really is. In some circles, the term seems to generate more heat than light.[1] The school from which I received my post-graduate counseling degree (and an additional post-graduate certificate) and at which I had to repeatedly defend the sufficiency of the Scriptures has now joined the bandwagon. Moreover, even among those adamantly against integrating clinical psychology into their counseling methodologies, there are significant differences in emphasis.[2]

Because of this obfuscation of the term *biblical counseling*, I have chosen to identify as a *historic* biblical counselor. There may be better, more politically correct ways to distinguish myself from those who do not hold to the sufficiency of Scripture, but for me, this is the clearest. So, what is the difference between a historic biblical counselor and one who claims to be a biblical (or Christian) counselor but does not believe the way I do?

---

1   I was recently invited to meet with a group of pastors abroad who had heard so many conflicting things about biblical counseling that they wanted clarification on over twenty issues. It took me almost three hours to address them all.

2   Perhaps most notably is "What is the greatest agent of change?" Is it the Spirit working through the Word, or is it the Spirit working through the loving relationship between the counselor and the person being counseled?

It's actually pretty simple to understand. A truly Christian (a biblical) counselor is one whose counseling model reflects the Scriptures *at every point*. A counselor who is a Christian uses a counseling model that does not reflect the Scriptures at every point. A Christian counselor presupposes only that which the Bible teaches. A counselor who is a Christian presupposes that which his favorite theory (or theories) teaches.

But why are a counselor's presuppositions so important?

The reason is that a counselor's presuppositions will ultimately dictate his or her philosophy and methodology of counseling.

Freudian counselors, for example, presuppose that individuals behave as they do because of something called an *unconscious mind*. This predisposes them to employ such methodologies as hypnosis, dream interpretation, free association (the uncensored and unsuppressed communication of whatever thoughts come to mind), and age regression.

Rogerian counselors presuppose that man, at the core of his being, is basically good and has within himself all the resources to solve his own problems. This predisposes them to give no direction but rather reflect back to the counselee, in paraphrases, the counselee's own words. Carl Roger (the founder of client-centered or person-centered counseling) has essentially redefined the word *counseling* (which hitherto meant "to give advice") in our society.

Adlerian counselors presuppose that man's two basic needs are security and significance. Many so-called Christian counselors believe that man lost both of these in the garden of Eden.

In his best-selling book, *The Search for Significance*, Dr. Robert McGee says about the fall, "To properly understand the devastating effects of this event, we need to examine the nature of man before sin caused him to lose his security and significance." McGee then goes on to read his Adlerian presupposition into the text, which, of course, mentions nothing about these two "basic needs."[3] This has predisposed some Christians who are counselors to encourage their counselees to seek after the wrong things. Rather than teaching them how to love God and love their neighbor as the Bible commands, these counselors inadvertently (or not) teach their counselees to love themselves by pursuing their own security and significance.

Not All Counselors Who Are Christian Are Christian Counselors

A counselor who is a Christian (but not a biblical counselor) uses a counseling model that does not reflect the Scriptures at every point. A *truly* Christian counselor builds his counseling model exegetically. He doesn't have a "counseling theory" but a "theology of counseling." A counselor who is a Christian supplements what the Bible has to say about changing people with so-called truth from other sources. One of the most significant differences between the two has to do with presuppositions. A Christian counselor presupposes only that which the Bible teaches. A counselor who is a Christian presupposes that which his favorite secular counseling theories (there are now hundreds from which to choose) teach.

The twelve presuppositions we will explore in this book were originally penned by Jay E. Adams.[4] They are not exhaustive, but I trust they will provide you with a framework by which you may discern whether the counsel you are giving (or receiving) is biblical.

---

3   Robert McGee, *The Search for Significance*, Rev. ed. (Nashville: Thomas Nelson, 2003), 13.
4   Jay E. Adams, *Update on Christian Counseling Volume 1* (Grand Rapids: Baker, 1980).

Presupposition 1

God Is in Control

O UR FIRST PRESUPPOSITION is a simple statement: **The God of the Bible is the sovereign creator and sustainer of the universe.**

Counseling usually involves helping people solve problems. That's why people most often come to see us. They need help with some difficulty that has befallen them—some conflict with another, some loss, a struggle with sin or painful emotion, or a set of circumstances they are having trouble resolving by themselves. They need help, and they need hope. Sometimes, they need more hope than help—especially toward the beginning of the counseling process. Helping people comprehend the sovereignty of God is one of the surest ways to offer people hope. To the degree that Christians believe that God is in control (that He is not asleep at the wheel), they will have hope. If they do not believe in the sovereignty of God—if they do not see His hand in the trial (if they think their problem has somehow taken God by surprise)—they will struggle to have hope.

What they must understand first and foremost is this: the sovereign creator and sustainer of the universe could remove the problem from the lives of His children (or have kept it from happening in the first place), but often, He chooses not to because

He is more interested in glorifying Himself and reproducing His character through their trials.[1]

If they are to have hope, they must come to see and really believe that God is bigger than their problem.[2] He is bigger than their difficult spouse, rebellious child, or unreasonable parent, teacher, or boss. He is bigger than their depression, anxiety, grief, or loneliness. He is bigger than their troubling circumstances, limited finances, or debilitating sickness. He is bigger than their life-dominating sin. Not only could He have prevented their problem from touching them, but He can also remove it or give them the grace to handle it going forward.

There is nothing that comes into the life of the Christian that the blessed and only Sovereign does not govern (1 Peter 6:15). (Read the first chapter of the book of Job again if you want to see this graphically illustrated.) One of my favorite Scripture passages on the sovereignty of God is Lamentations 3:37: "Who has spoken and it came to pass, unless the Lord has commanded it?" (ESV).

God is sovereign even over the sinful words and deeds of others. Jesus told Pontius Pilate, "You would have no authority over Me at all, unless it had been given you from above; for this reason the one who delivered Me over to you has the greater sin" (John 19:11).

God has purposes (good reasons) for allowing His children to go through trials. Some are temporal, and some are eternal. Consider the following:

> Consider it all joy, my brethren, when you encounter various trials, knowing that the testing of your faith produces endurance. And let endurance have its perfect result, so

---

1   Such Christians frequently lose sight of the fact that they are living in a sin-cursed world—that apart from the first and last two chapters of the Scripture, they will find that the world is dominated by sin, sickness, suffering, and Satan.

2   "And without faith it is impossible to please Him, for the one who comes to God must believe that He exists, and that He proves to be One who rewards those who seek Him" (Heb. 11:6).

that you may be perfect and complete, lacking in nothing. (James 1:2–4)

For momentary, light affliction is producing for us an eternal weight of glory far beyond all comparison, while we look not at the things which are seen, but at the things which are not seen; for the things which are seen are temporal, but the things which are not seen are eternal. (2 Cor. 4:17–18)

Beloved, do not be surprised at the fiery ordeal among you, which comes upon you for your testing, as though something strange were happening to you; but to the degree that you share the sufferings of Christ, keep on rejoicing, so that at the revelation of His glory you may also rejoice and be overjoyed. (1 Peter 4:12–13)

Christians who come to counseling must understand that God limits the trials in at least two ways. Notice the italicized words below:

No temptation has overtaken you except something common to mankind; and God is faithful, so He will *not allow you to be tempted beyond what you are able*, but with the temptation *will provide the way of escape also, so that you will be able to endure it*. (1 Cor. 10:13)

Sometimes, life appears to have us boxed in. It seems to those we are counseling that the walls are closing in around them. But if the counselee is a Christian, God promises to keep the walls from crushing him beyond his ability to handle it without sinning. The Lord knows how much temptation each of His children can handle and limits the trials and temptations accordingly. In addition, God also promises the Christian that someday He will get him out of the trial. It might be in this life, or it may be in the next, but God will deliver His children from temptation. Indeed, "the Lord knows how to rescue the godly from a trial" (2 Peter 2:9). Those you counsel will be tempted to extricate themselves from the box by utilizing sinful means and methods (such as divorce, suicide, manipulation, abuse of authority).[3] The question they must ask themselves (with a bit of prodding from you) is this: "Am I going to wait patiently for God to get me out of this box, or am I going to impatiently pull out my sinful little pocket knife and attempt to tunnel my way out of the box before God, through righteous means, extricates me in His own way?"

The Christian must remember that God is preparing him, while he is in the box, for what He has prepared for him once He lets him out of the box! It could, for example, be a future job, relationship, location, or ministry. The Father of mercies and God of all assistance "comforts us in all our affliction so that we will be able to comfort those who are in any affliction with the comfort with which we ourselves are comforted by God" (2 Cor.1:4).

I'll never forget sitting across the desk from a hurting counselee trying to minister to him when, suddenly, out of my mouth came the most spot-on, insightful counsel I had given in years. As I sat there amazed at what I was saying—knowing that through my words, the Spirit of God was pouring oil into the wounds of my hurting friend—my eyes began to water as I said in my heart, "Thank you, Lord—now I understand better than ever why I had to go through that horrible trial several years ago."[4]

I sometimes remind those I am trying to help that God will not allow anything to come into their lives beyond their control that will permanently hinder or damage His best for their lives. In fact, the purposes God has for trials and tribulations include our becoming more like Christ:

---

3   Sometimes, people turn to sinful ways of tranquilizing themselves while they are in the box (drugs, alcohol, pornography, self-mutilation, anorexic behavior, etc.), not realizing that these things not only close the walls around them even more but might actually hinder or retard God's desire to get them out of the box sooner rather than later.

4   From my book, *Resolving Conflict: How to Make Disturb and Keep Peace* (Phillipsburg, NJ: P&R, 2016), 84.

We know that God causes all things to work together for good to those who love God, to those who are called according to His purpose. For those whom He foreknew, *He also predestined to become conformed to the image of His Son,* so that He would be the firstborn among many brothers and sisters. (Rom. 8:28–29)

This leads to another area of God's sovereignty that counselees often need to be reminded of: His dominion over their sanctification (their growth into a mature Christian). Progressive sanctification is a work of God, but it is one in which we are enjoined to cooperate. However, God is often more committed to this process than we are (or at least than we realize).

The LORD *will accomplish what concerns me;* Your lovingkindness, O LORD, is everlasting; Do not forsake the works of Your hands. (Ps. 138:8)

So then, my beloved, just as you have always obeyed, not as in my presence only, but now much more in my absence, work out your own salvation with fear and trembling; *for it is God who is at work in you, both to will and to work for His good pleasure.* (Phil. 2:12–13)

For this reason I also suffer these things, but I am not ashamed; for I know whom I have believed and I am convinced that He is able to guard what I have entrusted to Him until that day. (2 Tim. 1:12; see also Eph. 3:20 and Jude 24)

God, through Christ, not only formed and fashioned the cosmos, but He also maintains and sustains it. There is not one radical molecule in the universe.[5] Those you counsel must be

---

5   R.C. Sproul said, "If there is one single molecule in this universe running around loose, totally free of God's sovereignty, then we have no guarantee that a single promise of God will ever be fulfilled." *Chosen by God* (Wheaton, IL: Tyndale Momentum, 1994).

convinced that God is in control of all things, including their lives, their circumstances, their families, their health, their futures—everything about them. Indeed, God is "the *blessed controller* of all things" (1 Tim. 6:15, PHILLIPS)!

Presupposition 2

——— MAN IS RESPONSIBLE ———

OUR SECOND PRESUPPOSITION, *Man was created in God's image as a responsible being,* directly contradicts most of the three hundred-plus counseling theories abroad in the culture. Most theories, in one way or another, declare or imply that man is not responsible for his actions. Indeed, they see each person as a victim of something or someone else. Freud says it is our parents' fault.[1] B.F. Skinner says the environment in which we grew up (or currently live) is the problem. Medical doctors often say it is either our DNA or brain chemistry that is to blame.[2]

---

1   I'll never forget a young woman I counseled my first year out of graduate school. She told me of her previous counselor who, at one point, instructed her saying, "Tell me that you hate your mother!" When she repeatedly said to the counselor in one way or another, "But I don't hate my mother," the counselor, in exasperation said, "Of course you hate her—you have to hate her because of all the terrible things she did to you!" That prompted her to look for another counselor.

2   There is one notable exception: William Glasser's Reality Therapy is a secular theory of counseling that actually does not allow its subjects to play the victim. Glasser effectively cleaned out a wing of the psychiatric ward of the hospital he was working at by holding people (and treating them as if they were) responsible for their actions. He would essentially tell them, "You're not sick; you're crazy. So, if you want to get out of this place, you better start taking responsibility for your actions."

While all these things may be contributing factors, they do not remove man's culpability before God. The Bible teaches that we sin because we are born sinners ("genetics"), are disposed to sin, and learn sinful patterns of behaviors from our parents and others (our environment) and that when our bodies are ill (our brain chemistry is out of whack), it is easier for us to sin and harder for us to obey God. Nevertheless, we may not blame our sins on these things. We may not adopt the mentality of a victim.

Despite the influence of these factors, we are responsible beings who will have to give an account of ourselves to a holy God. He holds us personally responsible for our behavior and expects us to change. (He also gives Christians the desire and power to do so, but that is another presupposition we will discuss later.) By *responsible*, I mean obedient to God's will. We may not excuse our behavior due to these "influences." We may not make excuses for our sinful thoughts, words, actions, and motives.

A biblical counselor must be adept at graciously disabusing people of their excuses. And there are a good many of them. Here are a few of the most popular:

- "I can't." As a Christian, you simply cannot say *can't* to something God has said you must do. You may say, "I won't," or "I don't want to," but the Bible says you can do (or at least learn to do) all things through Christ (Phil. 4:13).
- "I know what the Bible says but . . ." If the Bible says it, there are no buts about it. God will not ask you, if indeed you truly are a Christian, to do anything without giving you all the resources (i.e., the wisdom, the ability or grace, or even the desire) to do what He has asked.
- "I never had a good role model." You now have the role model of Jesus Christ (who has also given you His Word and His Spirit) to show you how to

change. Moreover, He has placed you in a church where there are others.

- **"My children (or spouse or parents)[3] provoke me into sinning. I can't change until they stop pushing my buttons."** Your response to others as a Christian is not dependent on their behavior toward you. Your love for them does not depend on their love for you. God's Word tells you to love not only your spouse and your neighbors but also your enemies (Matt. 5:43–48).[4] Indeed, you have been commanded, "Do not be overcome with evil, but overcome evil with good" (Rom. 12:21; see also vv. 17–20).
- **"I'm too old to change now—after all, 'You can't teach an old dog new tricks.'"** My typical response to this one is along these lines:

  I wouldn't know about that since I'm not a dog trainer. But you are not a dog but a human being made in the image of God who has the Holy Spirit residing in him. The Bible says Christians can and must (and therefore are able to) change at any age. Actually, it seems that older people are better adapted to change than younger ones are. God seems to save the most difficult changes for those who are older. Their bodies weaken and betray them, they are not as mobile and ambulatory as they once were, and they lose many of their friends, yet they are expected to adapt.

The people who hide behind these kinds of excuses are saying, in essence, "Please excuse me from living like a responsible adult before God because my case is different." But as we have seen, your counselee's case is *not* different. Although there are, no doubt, a few unique elements of his particular set of circumstances, all his

---

3 Or, for a man, those women who wear short skirts and tightfitting clothes.
4 Remember that *family members* are typically your closest neighbors.

problems are "common to man" (1 Cor. 10:13). God's grace (His supernatural power) is available to him if he is willing to avail himself of it.

But what keeps Christians from availing themselves of God's resources? Often it is laziness.[5] There is an interesting collation in Scripture between laziness and excuses:

> The *sluggard* says, "There is a lion outside;
> I will be killed in the streets!" (Prov. 22:13)

> The *sluggard* says, "There is a lion in the road!
> A lion is in the open square!"
> As the door turns on its hinges,
> So does the sluggard on his bed.
> The sluggard buries his hand in the dish;
> He is weary of bringing it to his mouth again.
> The *sluggard* is wiser in his own eyes
> Than seven men *who can give a discreet answer.* (Prov. 26:13–16)

> And the one also who had received the one talent came up and said, "Master, *I knew you to be a hard man, reaping where you did not sow and gathering where you scattered no seed. And I was afraid,* and went away and hid your talent in the ground. See, you have what is yours."

> But his master answered and said to him, "You wicked, *lazy* slave, you knew that I reap where I did not sow and gather where I scattered no seed. Then you ought to have put my money in the bank, and on my arrival I would have received my money back with interest. Therefore take away the talent from him, and give it to the one who has the ten talents." (Matt. 25:24–28)

Christians who do not act responsibly do not function at the optimum level of efficiency God intends for them. Those

---

5 There are other obstacles to grace such as pride (James 4:6) and fear (Matt. 25:24–28).

who routinely give into their feelings sooner or later give up on their responsibilities. The mental, emotional, and physical consequences they experience grow worse. As time goes by, the excuses they use to justify themselves to themselves and to others become more and more convincing in their own minds. (Rather than interpreting the excuses as excuses, they increasingly view them as the *cause* of their problems.)

The Image of God

On the bookshelf behind my desk is a framed photograph of my wife in her wedding dress. To most people, it is really just a piece of paper behind a piece of glass. They hardly notice it. But when I look at it, it is more than just a piece of glossy paper. It is quite precious. It is valuable because of the image the paper bears. The photo represents a special person, someone with whom I've shared my life for over thirty years. So, as you can imagine, I would not take kindly to someone who threw that little picture frame on the ground and stomped on it, even though I could replace it for just a few dollars.

Every human being bears the image of God. Yes, that image was very much distorted by the fall, but it still is a representation of the Creator and, as such, should be shown respect.

Part of man's redemption is the restoration of that Image. It will be completed in the new creation (heaven), but the process begins with the Holy Spirit's sanctifying work on earth. This is the goal of every true Christian counselor.

Into what do you suppose secular approaches to counseling try to turn their counselees? Jay Adams would liken the process of biblical counseling to that of making sausage. The counselor has a magic sausage grinder that can produce almost any type of sausage imaginable. A seemingly endless variety of sausages is made around the world. I've eaten them in England, Germany, Italy, Portugal, Austria, Switzerland, Brazil, Mexico, Japan, and throughout the United States. I've eaten hot sausages, spicy sausages, mild sausages, sweet sausages, thick sausages, thin sausages, pork sausages, venison sausages, chicken sausages, turkey sausages, and lamb sausages. I've even attempted to make sausage myself.

So, the question becomes, If all counselors are trying to bring about change, what are they changing their subjects into? That is, what kind of sausage are they going to make, and who decides what the sausage that comes out of the sausage machine looks like?

Unlike the Skinnerian therapist, who imposes his own subjective standards on his client and determines for himself what he will turn his client into, and unlike the Rogerian, who allows his client to determine for himself what he would like to become, and unlike many other therapists, who use similar subjective means to determine what is and what is not appropriate behavior, the Christian counselor has as his primary focus the objective and the eternal goal of reproducing the character of Jesus Christ in his counselee.

> My children, with whom I am again in labor until Christ is formed in you. (Gal 4:19)

> We proclaim Him, admonishing every man and teaching every man with all wisdom, so that we may present every man complete in Christ. (Col. 1:28)

One final thought: while changing people is one of the goals of Christian counseling, it is not the ultimate goal. The ultimate end of everything the Christian does is the glory of God: "Whether, then, you eat or drink or whatever you do, do all to the glory of God" (1 Cor. 10:31). That means the motives of the counselee and the counselor should be examined regularly throughout the counseling process.

Presupposition 3

CONNECTING THE DOTS
BETWEEN SIN AND MISERY

PEOPLE DO NOT ALWAYS appreciate that the pain they experience is often due to acting or thinking in ways out of harmony with Scripture. Biblical counselors, therefore, must understand the relationship between *sin* and *misery*.

Our third presupposition has to do with the link between these two realities: **Sin, which is thinking or acting independently of God, results in misery, both temporal and eternal.**

Many of the over three hundred secular counseling models would agree with the humanist manifesto that denies the existence of consequences for sin. But the Bible declares, "God is not mocked; for whatever a man sows, this he will also reap" (Gal. 6:7; see also Eph. 4:18; Rom. 8:20; Lam. 3:39; Matt. 25:41; 2 Thess. 1:9).

The Westminster Confession of Faith puts it well:

> Every sin, both original and actual, being a transgression of the righteous law of God, and contrary thereunto, doth, in its own nature, bring guilt upon the sinner, whereby he is bound over to the wrath of God, and curse of the law, and so made subject to death, with all miseries spiritual, temporal, and eternal.

Many counselees fail to connect their sin with the misery that impelled them into your office. It is your job to connect the dots for them.[1]

God's laws are non-optional. No one, regardless of his religious disposition, can violate them without suffering the consequences. If I, as a born-again Christian, were to jump off the Empire State Building, God's universal, non-optional law of gravity would impel me toward Fifth Avenue, and I would suffer the earth-splattering consequences of violating this precept. And if my Buddhist, Muslim, or atheistic friends followed suit, they would suffer the same tragic consequence. No matter who you are, you cannot violate God's laws and expect to avoid some degree of misery.

Part of your task as a counselor is to help the counselee clearly see the relationship between his misery and the unbiblical thoughts, motives, words, and actions that cause it. Sometimes, the relationship is apparent to both of you. Sometimes, neither of you has an immediate, clear understanding of the cause and effect between the two. That is why you must prayerfully depend on the Word and the Spirit to help you explore the counselee's problems and carefully connect the dots. You must be sure you do not connect dots that shouldn't be connected. To be sure, all misery is the result of sin. But all the misery your counselee is experiencing is not necessarily the result of his *own* sin. Do not make the correlation definitively unless you are certain one exists. Remember Job's three friends, the grief they caused him, and the wrath to which their unbiblical counsel provoked God (Job 42:7–9).

Sometimes, you may only be able to suggest the possibility of the sin/misery dynamic, encouraging the counselee to assess for

---

1   Although this point will be covered in a separate presupposition, it is worth mentioning here that it is necessary to point out to some counselees the *eternal* consequences of sin. Counselees who do not know Christ will have to be evangelized *before* real biblical change can occur. This "pre-counseling" is necessary because a person cannot be biblically counseled apart from the quickening of the Holy Spirit.

himself the likelihood of the connection.[2] You might say, "Have you thought about the possibility that your depression *could* be the result of your unwillingness to forgive your boss?" Or perhaps, "The Bible teaches that God disciplines those He loves. Could it be that you are being disciplined by God and are despising (thinking lightly of) His chastisement?"

This presupposition defines sin as disobedience, which is acting or thinking independently from God. In the garden of Eden, before being tempted to believe that it would be better to think or act autonomously, man was totally dependent on God's Word for direction. But he chose not to follow the divine directions he was given. Consequently, sin entered the human race. This desire to think and act independently from God (with all its intrinsic misery) is now locked into man's heart from birth (really, from the womb; see Ps. 51:1). Only Christ can free him from it. And even then, freedom will not be completely experienced in this life.

We often think of our thoughts as being very distinct from our behaviors. But from God's point of view, thinking is a form of behavior—it's an action of our minds. And as such, it has the capability of being sinful. Sinful thinking carries consequences: "The backslider in heart will have his fill of his own ways" (Prov. 14:14).

---

2   Counselors will have to enlist the help of those they counsel to verify possible tentative mental attitude diagnoses—those having to do with thoughts and motives of the heart. Care should be taken to not assertively, categorically, or emphatically suggest diagnosis to the counselee about matters of his heart. You may have to resist the temptation to get an immediate diagnosis but rather wait until the counselee has the time and biblical resources to consider what you are suggesting. (Be on guard also against the temptation to show off your diagnostic prowess to your counselee, remembering that it is the Lord who has given you such wisdom, not to enhance your own reputation but that you might glorify Him with it.) I will typically say to my counselee, "I can't see what is in your heart, so you will have to prayerfully look in there and tell me what is going on. Have you considered that this might be a matter of pride (or selfishness, rebellion, people-pleasing, love of money, or 'whatever'?")

Your counselee can talk to himself at over twelve hundred words per minute—especially when he is under stress or experiencing emotional distress.[3] He can tell himself a dozen lies in thirty seconds. How often have you counseled a spouse who said, "If I don't get out of this marriage, I'm going to go crazy"? Has that counselee considered that the likelihood of going crazy is much greater by stepping out of God's revealed will, by initiating an unbiblical divorce, than by suffering in it? Obviously not. That's where you must open your Bible and connect the dots for him (or, as is more apt to be the case, for her). How many depressed people have you seen whose depression resulted from bitter, angry, or anxious thoughts? And how about those who are depressed because of wrong values—they love things God says they shouldn't love, and they don't love what He says they should. They want things God doesn't want them to have, and they value those things He doesn't (and undervalue the things He does). They seek their rewards in this life rather than in the next. Why are they so miserable? It's because the thoughts and intents of their hearts are sinful.

Most Christians can clearly see the connection between sinful actions and distressing emotions (i.e., the adulterer facing intense grief and loneliness that resulted from his wife leaving him; the angry parent dealing with the guilt, sorrow, and embarrassment that accompanies having to parent a child who has been provoked to characterological anger; or the Xanex-addicted wife whose illegal "doctor shopping" has landed her in jail, totally isolated from her loved ones.). But many fail to consider the relationship between their sinful thoughts and the emotional misery such malefic mental activity often brings.

God has placed within the human body a capacity to experience pain. He also put in the spirit of man the capability to trigger painful emotions such as anxiety, fear, bitterness, loneliness, guilt,

---

3   This is especially true when his adrenal glands are releasing adrenalin into his blood stream because of the way he is responding to his environment in his heart (the way he is interpreting it to himself).

depression, rejection, and despair. There is a positive function for these "negative" emotions.[4]

Most Americans would not seek the help of a physician unless they were in some kind of bodily pain. Physical pain, therefore, can be a good thing because it tells us something is wrong. Similarly, most counselees would not seek the help of a counselor unless they were in some kind of emotional distress. Pain, then, should be viewed as a symptom. It is God's way of letting us know something may be wrong in our lives that must be remedied.

Here is how I sometimes explain this dynamic to my counselees.[5]

Imagine lying in bed at 3:30 a.m. when, suddenly, your smoke detector startles you from a wonderful dream.[6] How dare that obnoxious little plastic gadget wake you up out of a sound sleep by piercing the night with its cacophonous 95-decibel distress signal! How will you ever get back to sleep with that continuous piercing alarm screaming in your ears?

"We'll just see about that!" you mutter to yourself as you jam your fingers into your ears, pull the pillow around the back of your head, and try to fall back to sleep.

After five or six minutes of torment, you unplug your ears and grope around under your bed for the nearest shoe. Then you throw off the covers, jump out of bed, stomp off toward the smoke detector with boot in hand, and begin to smash it to smithereens.

"That's absurd!" says the counselee.

---

4   We perceive them as negative because of their distressing nature. The emotions themselves are technically not negative but natural—that is, they are experienced the way God intended when we do or fail to do those things that violate His will.

5   Adapted from my book, *Picking up the Pieces* (Phillipsburg, NJ: P&R, 2012).

6   I'm indebted to Dr. Wayne Mack for first "awakening me" to the smoke-detector illustration.

"Why is that absurd?" I ask.

"Because the real problem is not with the smoke detector. It's with the fire that set off the smoke detector."

"Exactly! It is foolish to smash the smoke detector when it's doing what it was designed to do and is working only too well."

Yet, this is often how people deal with their emotions. They ignore them, hoping the pain will go away. Or they turn to alcohol, run to the psychiatrist's office for some pill (or perhaps something more radical like electro-shock therapy), or do whatever else it takes to make the pain (misery) go away, without giving any thought as to whether their sinful behavior might be a factor. In their desperation, they never stop to consider that the real problem may not be with their emotions but with some "fire" in their lives. Why? Because they have not been taught to relate the misery in their lives (which they wrongly see as the real problem) to their sinful thoughts.

"Are you saying that all painful emotions are the result of one's sin?"

Certainly not! All misery, including most pain, is the result of sin, but as I've already pointed out, not all pain is the result of *our own* sin. Christ was without sin, yet He was "a man of sorrows and acquainted with grief" (Isa. 53:3; see also Matt. 26:38). He said, "Blessed are those who mourn" (Matt. 5:4). He could "sympathize with our weaknesses" (Heb. 4:15). He became angry (Mark 3:5) and indignant (Mark 10:14).[7] He wept over the death of His friend (John 11:34–35) and the city of Jerusalem (Luke 19:41).

Since Jesus Christ was perfect and could not sin, He never experienced any emotion that was the result of His own sin—He never needed an emotional smoke detector to alert Him to personal wrongdoing. You and I, however, often experience feelings that warn us about sin in our lives.

---

7   In his Gospel, Mark uses at least four different Greek words to describe the Lord's anger.

It is clear, then, that not all potentially distressing emotions are the result of personal sin. They may simply be the normal result of adjusting to new and stressful circumstances. They may be attributed to physiological causes such as illness or fatigue. Do not ignore such factors as these when considering the potential causes of distressing emotions in those you minister to. Often, the unhappiness your counselees experience is the result of several converging factors.

The chart that follows is a page from a Christian's owner's manual (well, actually, it's a page from an *imaginary* manual, based on the Bible, of course, that a Christian might consult when his feelings start causing trouble). It explains how a person may read his on-board "emotion detection device." The chart can be used in much the same way as the troubleshooting guide that comes with your car, computer, or microwave oven. The first column names the siren, or painful emotion, a Christian may be experiencing. The second column alerts him to what might be causing the alarm to go off.

Emotional Troubleshooting Guide[8]

Sinful Anger

- I may not have submitted my desires to God.
- I may be complaining against God for how He ordains my life's circumstances.
- I may be guilty of idolatry (loving something more than God).
- I may be focusing more on that which is temporal than that which is eternal.

Fear

- I may not love God as I should.[9]

---

8   Priolo, *Picking up the Pieces*, 36–37.
9   First John 4:18 teaches that one's love for God (and apprehension of God's love for him) casts out fear.

- I may not trust God as I should.
- I may not love my neighbor as I should.
- I may be focusing on myself more than on my responsibilities.

Loneliness

- I may be expecting others, rather than God, to meet my needs.
- I may not be enjoying the companionship of my best friend (the Holy Spirit).
- It may be that I am not spending enough time in Bible study, prayer, or Christian fellowship.
- I may be limiting my friendships by my unwillingness to let God choose my friends based on how I can minister to them.

Anxiety

- I may not trust God as I should.
- I may have a temporal value system (What am I afraid of losing?).
- I may be guilty of sinful thoughts or actions I have not repented of.

Depression

- I may be worrying about something.
- I may not have adequately dealt with guilt.
- I may not have forgiven someone who hurt me.
- I may not have been fulfilling my biblical responsibilities.
- I may be mishandling a trial or excessively grieving over something God has removed from my life.
- I may be wanting or loving something more than God wants me to.

Excessive Sorrow

- I may love (have loved) that which I lost more than I love God.
- I may not be focusing my thoughts on the right things.
- I may be focusing more on what I have lost than on whom I should love.

Jealousy

- I may be looking to someone other than God to meet my needs.
- I may be focusing on how someone is not loving me rather (or more) than on how I can love that person.
- I may have a temporal value system.
- I may not be rejoicing with those who rejoice.

Bitterness[10]

- I may not have forgiven someone who hurt me.
- I may have failed to confront my offender biblically.
- I may not be overcoming evil with good (Rom. 12:21).
- I may be focusing more on the person who offended me than I am on glorifying my Sovereign Lord, who (for His wise purposes) allowed the offense into my life.

Since the suggestions I've listed are far from exhaustive, you may wonder how to figure out which option(s) apply to your counselee. That's where the Bible comes in. "The word of God . . . is a discerner of the thoughts and intents of the heart" (Heb. 4:12 NKJV). Encourage your counselee to prayerfully use the Scriptures to discern the cause of the problem—not in words taught

---

10   This is such a common counseling issue (one that is very misunderstood due to much erroneous teaching in recent years) that I wrote a booklet to help those I counsel understand it properly, entitled *Bitterness: The Root that Pollutes* (Phillipburg, NJ: P&R, 2008). A booklet in that series addresses fear as well: *Fear: Breaking Its Grip*.

by human wisdom but by the Spirit, expressing spiritual truths in spiritual words (1 Cor. 2:13). Remember, you can't see what's in his heart. His words, actions, and attitudes, however, are fair game for you to judge (biblically discern); his thoughts and motives are not (1 Cor. 4:5). Give him the tools, show him how to use them, and then urge him to look into his own heart.

I sometimes use a diagram to help people I'm working with connect the dots between their heartaches and their sinful thoughts and actions. I explain, "Your unbiblical thoughts (and desires) usually have as one of their natural consequences misery (including distressing emotions). Let's suppose that you have a feeling-oriented view of forgiveness, and so you decide to wait until you *feel* forgiveness for your offender before you forgive him. Rather than going to him as the Lord prescribed in Luke 17:3 or overlooking his sin, according to Proverbs 19:11, you start to ruminate on the offense. In the meantime, you tell yourself, 'I'm just not ready to forgive John yet!' This thought, along with the continuous reviewing of the offense, produces the distressing emotion of bitterness in your heart. Here is what happens:[11]

THOUGHTS

EMOTIONS

"Your unforgiving thoughts produce feelings of bitterness."

---

11   Bitterness is the result of dwelling too long on a hurt. It is cultivating an offense by repeatedly reviewing it in one's mind until a root of bitterness sprouts and grows into a fully developed weed (see Heb. 15:12).

But it may not end there. Suppose you allow that thought process to germinate not only into bitterness but also into an overt act of revenge. Perhaps you slander him or detract from his 'good name' in some other way or give him the 'silent treatment.' Now, in addition to bitterness (and depending on your conscience, perhaps a lesser amount of guilt), there is bitterness and a greater measure of guilt—a conscience that is not free from offense either toward God or man (see Acts 24:16) and will not stop nagging until you seek forgiveness from your offender for your retaliatory action. Here's what that dynamic looks like:

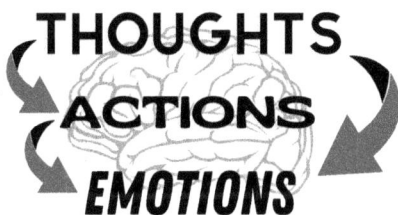

THOUGHTS
ACTIONS
EMOTIONS

"Your vindictive actions that flow from your unforgiving thoughts produce feelings of guilt. So, sinful contemplations produce misery directly, and they may lead to sinful words and actions that also produce misery."

But why talk about misery to the counselee? What's the point of cursing the darkness when all you have to do is turn on the light? Sometimes, counselees are convinced the problem is something other than sin. In such cases, connecting the dots for the counselee will give him hope. Take, for example, a depressed person who has been told he is suffering from a chemical imbalance. (Of course, no blood was ever drawn or sent to a laboratory to substantiate the diagnosis, let alone to determine scientifically the exact chemicals that are out of whack. Instead, a series of questions about the patient's feelings were administered verbally, and the Diagnostic and Statistical Manual of Mental Disorders (DSM-5) disease diagnosis was made with the cockiness that only a medical school graduate can exude.[12] And then, medication was prescribed to correct the "imbalance" whose exact chemical function inside the brain even its manufacturer admits is uncertain.) Here's how a biblical counselor might connect the dots if he sees a clear correlation between the counselee's sin and misery:

"Sally, I'm not a physician and do not claim to be an expert in psychopharmacology, but on the basis of what you told me, several things are going on in your life that could be contributing to your depression above and beyond any organic problems your doctor may find.[13] First, you told me you are struggling with *bitterness* toward your husband. Second, you explained that you feel very *guilty* because your bitterness has prevented you from loving him in at least three ways. And then you admitted that you *worry* about how much your resentment toward your husband negatively affects your children. I can tell you that bitterness, guilt (over sin that has not been confessed and forsaken), and anxiety all have, as a consequence, depression. Let me show you in the Bible why these things are so."

At this point, you can paint a vivid picture of the sin/misery dynamic that the counselee can carry around with him by unpacking portions of passages such as Psalm 32 or 38.[14]

---

12   Just kidding—some of my best friends are doctors (humble ones) . . . really!

13   Then there's the whole question of which came first, the chemical imbalance or the sin (every time you stub your toe, the chemicals in your brain go "out of balance"), but we'll save that for another chapter.

14   The purpose for this is not simply to make him more aware of his own culpability but to motivate him to avoid making the same miserable mistakes in the future. Some counselees will also have to be instructed on "how to deal with guilt" by properly apprehending and appropriating God's forgiveness

When I kept silent about my sin, my body wasted away
Through my groaning all day long.
For day and night Your hand was heavy upon me;
My vitality was drained away as with the fever heat of
summer. Selah. . . .

Many are the sorrows of the wicked,
But he who trusts in the LORD, lovingkindness shall sur-
round him. (Ps. 32:3–4, 10)

"Brenda, could it be that the reason you are depressed is that
you have been keeping silent about your sin (you have not confessed and forsaken it)?"

O LORD, rebuke me not in Your wrath,
And chasten me not in Your burning anger.
For Your arrows have sunk deep into me,
And Your hand has pressed down on me.
There is no soundness in my flesh because of Your indigna-
tion;
There is no health in my bones because of my sin.
For my iniquities are gone over my head;
As a heavy burden, they weigh too much for me.
My wounds grow foul and fester
Because of my folly.
I am bent over and greatly bowed down;
I go mourning all day long.
For *my loins are filled with burning,*
And *there is no soundness in my flesh.*
I am benumbed and badly crushed;
I groan because of the agitation of my heart.

Lord, all my desire is before You;
And my sighing is not hidden from You.
My heart throbs, my strength fails me;
And *the light of my eyes, even that has gone from me.*

---

through Christ's atoning sacrifice. Psalms 51 and 103 are especially helpful
for this.

My loved ones and my friends stand aloof from my plague;
And my kinsmen stand afar off.
Those who seek my life lay snares for me;
And those who seek to injure me have threatened destruction,
And they devise treachery all day long. . . .
For I am ready to fall,
And my sorrow is continually before me.
For *I confess my iniquity;*
I am full of anxiety because of my sin. (Ps. 38:1–12, 17–18)

"Jim, have you ever stopped to consider that the physical problems you are experiencing might somehow be connected to those sinful thoughts and actions you've been telling me about?"

Another reason to discuss with the counselee his misery has to do with conviction. "The Scriptures are useful for . . . conviction" (2 Tim. 3:16). Sometimes, you, like Timothy, must convict your counselees of their sin to help motivate them to change. How many things would you change in your life if it were *not* a sin *not* to change? Christians must usually be convicted of sin before they are willing to invest the amount of time, effort, and thought required to replace one habit with another. (Take a look at what the Lord said to the Laodacians and the order in which He said it: "Those whom I love I *convict* . . . so *repent*" [Rev. 3:19].) The Bible is replete with useful (rebuking, exhorting, convicting) passages that show the relationship between sin and suffering. Become familiar with them. Learn to explain what they mean in easy-to-understand language, how to illustrate them in contemporary terms, and how to apply them in a variety of counseling circumstances.

I'm fairly confident that the old adage "misery loves company" is not theologically accurate. But, in one sense, we can say with biblical certainty that "misery *has* company"—the sinful thoughts, desires, words, actions, and attitudes that often accompany it. This week, your job may well be to acquaint your counselee's misery with his company.

Presupposition 4

———— THE BIBLE AND PSYCHOLOGY ————

IS THE BIBLE A TEXTBOOK for psychology? If you were to walk into a psychology class at many of our Christian universities and ask this question, you would find a significant number of people on both sides of this issue. In fact, professors on the same faculty often differ on this very fundamental question.

"How can that be?"

It has to do with our fourth presupposition: **The Bible is the only complete and authoritative textbook written specifically to provide the answers to both man's behavioral problems and the means for man's behavioral changes.** What's more, as someone who counsels biblically (or wants to learn how to do so), you ought to know how to answer this question. To a large degree, your ability to provide help and hope to your counselee depends on it.

Before Sigmund Freud arrived on the scene, where do you suppose people turned when they needed "psychological" help?

Not sure?

Then, where did God expect people to turn when they needed "psychological" help before Freud?

The answer shouldn't surprise you.

Before Freud, ministers of the gospel were the primary source of such help. Back then, a pastor could not cop out of his pastoral responsibilities by sending his parishioners to the psychiatrist, many of whom cop out (or justify their unwillingness to really counsel their patients because of the high costs typically associated with their services) by sending their patients to the pharmacist). Back then, ministers were the experts.

In case you doubt this, look at what Eric Fromm, one of Freud's followers, wrote:

> Freud's method, psychoanalysis, made possible the most minute and intimate study of the soul. . . . The analyst is not a theologian or a philosopher and does not claim competence in those fields; but as a physician of the soul, he is concerned with the very same problems as philosophy and theology: the soul of man and its cure.
>
> If we thus define the function of the psychoanalyst, we find that at present two professional groups are concerned with the soul: the priests and the psychoanalysts.[15]

Freud knew exactly what he was doing. He determined to compete with Christianity for the solutions to life's problems. (In 1886, as an apparent act of defiance, he opened his private practice on *Easter Sunday*.) And that is perhaps the greatest danger of psychology as we know it today: it is *competitive* with Christianity. In towns and cities across America (and around the globe), psychiatrists and psychologists have gone into business for the express purpose of doing one thing: helping people *change*. Yet, changing people is the work of the Holy Spirit. Changing people is the function of Scripture. Changing people is the job of the church of Jesus Christ.

Freud died in 1939, but in 1933, John Dewey and company signed the Humanist Manifesto, thus encouraging these

---

15   Erich Fromm, *Psychoanalysis and Religion* (New York: Bantam, 1967), 7.

pseudo-soul doctors to develop and propagate their theories. Today, more than three hundred of these competitive and often contradictory psychotherapies exist. Most of the people in your church (and others to whom you minister) have been counseled by "professionals" in your community who have been trained in some of these theories. This is true even for the majority of so-called Christian counselors.

Psychobabble

The impact of humanism on psychology is undeniable. Perhaps the best way to demonstrate this is to examine the *language* of psychotherapy. But first, another question: How is it that many Christians view psychology as something foreign to Scripture? That is, why is psychology seen as something outside the realm of God's Word?

Most of us have come to associate psychology with terms and ideas not found in the Bible. Words like *schizophrenia, paranoia, neurosis, transference, ego, operant conditioning, defense mechanisms, self-actualization,* and *codependency* have filled our minds and clouded the issues. But this fuzzy thinking is not how it should be for people who interpret life from God's point of view. Scripture maintains that Christians should avoid the use of words and terminology of this world system whenever biblical concepts will suffice:

> Now we have received, not the spirit of the world, but the Spirit who is from God, so that we might know the things freely given to us by God, which things we also speak, not in words taught by human wisdom, *but in those taught by the Spirit, combining spiritual thoughts with spiritual words.* (1 Cor. 2:12–13)

The logical fallacy goes something like this: The word *kleptomania* is not found in the Bible. *Kleptomania* is a psychological word. Therefore, the Bible is not a textbook for psychology.

The term *codependency* is not found in the Bible. *Codependency* is a psychological term. Therefore, again, the Bible is not a textbook for psychology.

Much of today's psychological jargon reflects humanistic presuppositions and has connotations that oppose the Scriptures. Our culture has redefined what God has called sin as "disease" or "genetic predisposition" or any number of other "disorders" that abolish human responsibility and declare man a victim of circumstance.[16] A kleptomaniac is another way to say *thief.* Codependency is another way (man's way) of classifying the sin of inordinate people pleasing.[17]

Not only has psychology reclassified sinful behavior into respectable categories but it has also redefined the human personality. First Corinthians 2:13 also applies to biblical anthropology. We need not invent categories of human personality and, alongside them, additional corresponding problems. If Scripture does not address the subject—because a particular construct either does not exist or is called by another name—then why complicate the matter?[18] God's view of that nonmaterial part of man is frequently quite different from the fabrication of man.

---

16   For an interesting perspective on how the DSM series has progressively made it possible for people who commit crimes to escape culpability, see Thomas Szasz, *The Myth of Mental Illness* (New York: Harpercollins World, 2010). Another fascinating book about the history of the DSM and how it has gone from being a cause-and-effect based diagnostic to a symptom-based one is Gary Greenburg, *The Book of Woe: The DSM and The Unmasking of Psychiatry* (n.p.: Blue Rider, 2013).

17   For more about this, see my book *Pleasing People: How to Not Be an Approval Junkie* (Phillipsburg, NJ: P&R, 2007).

18   Adding to biblical anthropology (especially by inventing additional organs of the soul) beyond what Scripture allows can not only muddy the water and confuse (obfuscate things in the mind of those you are trying to help) but may also lead to unbiblical solutions that address problems that don't exist.

What Is Psychology?

There are two basic kinds of psychology. Failure to distinguish between these two will make a proper answer to our question about the Bible being a textbook for psychology very difficult.

Let's begin by looking at the etymology of the word *psychology*. It is a compound word formed from two Greek words: *psyche* and *logos*. *Logos* is the Greek term for "word." But in English usage, when a substantive ends with this *-ology* suffix, it generally means "the study of." Psychology, then, is the study of the "psyche" (whatever that is!). Interestingly, this word, *psyche*, appears more than one hundred times in the Greek New Testament. Of those occurrences, it has been translated as "life" forty times and "soul" fifty-eight times. Psychology, then, strictly (etymologically) speaking, is the study of the soul.

If psychology is the study of the soul, it would follow that psychiatry (from the Greek word *iasthai*, "to heal") is the medical treatment of the soul.

Descriptive vs. Prescriptive

The distinction that must be maintained between the two branches of psychology is the difference between *descriptive* psychology and *counseling* (or clinical) psychology. One involves the study of the soul; the other involves its cure. One merely *describes* human behavior; the other *prescribes* its therapy. The first seeks to *recognize* human behavior; the last seeks to *remedy* it. The first falls more in line with the etymological definition of psychology; the second with the etymological definition of psychiatry. The former, if done properly, does not necessarily compete with Christianity. The latter necessarily does!

Describing human behavior does not necessarily compete with the Bible because the Bible does not claim to be a book that describes every aspect of every human behavior.[19] It does not, for

---

19　It describes human behavior sufficiently to help us make a biblical diagnosis of all nonorganic problems resulting from sin.

example, explain at what approximate age children's thought patterns change from basically concrete to more abstract in nature. Neither does it explain all the apparent differences between the sexes. In this regard, then, the Bible is not, strictly speaking, a textbook for psychology.

Although the Bible has much to say concerning human behavior, it has not been given primarily for that purpose. Since it does address this issue, however, it ought to be the first book consulted by Christian descriptive psychologists so that biblical terminology can be employed to describe those behaviors defined in Scripture "not with the words that man's wisdom teaches, but that which the Holy Spirit teaches."

Now, what about counseling or clinical psychology? Is the Bible a textbook for this "prescriptive" (soul care) kind of psychology?

While it is true that the Bible makes no claims to function exclusively as a systematic all-inclusive manual for classifying human behavior, that it claims to function as a *counseling textbook* cannot be denied. We will look at three such claims.

Qualification One

The Bible qualifies as a textbook for counseling because it was given to thoroughly equip the minister of the gospel to perform his pastoral duties (which include counseling): "All Scripture is God-breathed and is profitable for teaching, reproving, correcting and training in righteousness, so that the man of God may be complete, thoroughly equipped for every good work" (2 Tim. 3: 16–17). The term "man of God" used by Paul in the Pastoral Epistles is borrowed from the Old Testament prophets. In the New Testament, it is a synonym for *pastor*. Paul is telling Timothy that the Scriptures are able to equip him *totally* for each ministry he will ever have to perform. Counseling is clearly one of those good works Paul had in mind when he wrote these assuring words to Pastor Timothy.

"Yes, but aren't some problems too deep for a pastor to handle?"

Those problems are usually too deep for a pastor *not* to handle:

> For the word of God is alive and powerful, and sharper than any two-edged sword, piercing even to the division of soul and spirit. (Heb. 4:12a NKJV)

You cannot get to a deeper part of human personality than the division of soul and spirit. That is, you cannot penetrate (pierce) more precisely to a deeper level of the human psyche than the place where the soul and spirit come together (or meet).

> And is [Scripture] the discerner of the thoughts and intents of the heart. (Heb. 4:12b NKJV)

You cannot get to a *deeper* level of human motivation than the *thoughts* and *intents* (or motives) of the heart. You cannot diagnose the *musings* and *motives* of man's heart with precision apart from the Word of God. Only a man of God equipped with Scripture can discern those deeper thoughts and motivations. All that is necessary to equip the pastor to fulfill his ministry of changing people is found in the Bible.

Qualification Two

The Bible qualifies as a textbook for counseling because, throughout it, God "granted to us everything pertaining to life and godliness, through the true knowledge of"[20]

Sigmund Freud?

Albert Ellis?

B. F. Skinner?

Carl Rogers?

Dr. Laura?

Dr. Phil?

20   2 Peter 1:3

No! God has given us these resources for change "through the true knowledge of Him who called us by His own glory and excellence."

> Grace and peace be multiplied to you in the knowledge of God and of Jesus our Lord; seeing that His divine power has granted to us everything pertaining to life and godliness, through the true knowledge of Him who called us by His own glory and excellence. For by these He has granted to us His precious and magnificent promises, so that by them you may become partakers of the divine nature, having escaped the corruption that is in the world by lust. (2 Peter 1:2–4)

In other words, through the knowledge of Jesus Christ, the Wonderful Counselor, God has provided everything we need to solve problems of living and problems stemming from ungodliness.

Furthermore, the next verse explains that through these exceeding great and precious promises, we may become partakers of the divine nature (share with God His communicable attributes) and thereby escape the moral corruption that is in the world through lust.

Did Dr. Freud have the tools to produce this nature in his patients and so enable them to escape (flee from) sin's grasp? Are Ellis's needs of *security* and *significance* more basic to man's well-being than the need to love God and love others? Can Skinner, by operant or classical conditioning, produce in his clients the fruit of the Spirit? Will Rogers's non-directive approach to counseling enable us to present every man complete in Christ? Will Dr. Laura's and Dr. Phil's best-selling books have the sanctifying impact on the people you counsel as will the Scriptures? Did the Wonderful Counselor rely on anything but knowledge of Scripture and the power of God to transform people's lives?

Of course not! That takes a nature fashioned by God—a divinely given one!

The three most effective dynamics of change known to man are not the product of any human counselor. Do you know what they are?

1. The Holy Spirit
2. The Word of God
3. The local church

The vast majority of psychological textbooks ignore these dynamics, and some discredit them.

Qualification Three

The Bible qualifies as a textbook for counseling because it is comprehensive and perfect in its capacity to restore man's soul: "The law of the LORD is perfect [complete], restoring the soul" (Ps. 19:7). This verse was hand-painted on a welcome sign at the front door of the counseling center where I worked for years. It is the motto of my ministry. It has motivated me since graduate school.

You see, we Christian counselors have only begun to scratch the surface of Scripture when it comes to finding lasting solutions to life's problems. I have committed my life to researching Scripture for the antidotes to sin that so many of my colleagues are searching for outside of Scripture—and by God's grace, I am finding them!

I once had a graduate professor of a Christian college tell me that, in his opinion, over 75 percent of the undergraduate students majoring in psychology at that school were studying psychology to find answers to problems in their own lives. The tragedy of this fact is not that these students are looking for solutions to their problems but that so many Christian young people are studying *psychology* rather than *theology* to solve their problems. They simply do not have confidence in the sufficiency of Scripture to provide those solutions. In other words, the tragedy is that they are turning to man rather than God for help.

The law of the Lord is perfect in its ability to provide whatever it takes to restore the nonorganic, psychological part of man. The Hebrew word for *perfect* is *tamim*: complete, comprehensive, all-inclusive.[21] The Hebrew word for *restore* is *shiba*: to convert or repent. In other words, the Bible is completely sufficient in its capacity to supply the Christian with the material necessary to be transformed into the image of the Lord Jesus Christ.

Now What Do You Think?

Is the Bible a textbook for counseling? It is. Don't be intimidated by the competition—there really is none! Nothing on this earth can compete with the life-transforming power of the Holy Spirit, the Word of God, and the local church. My prayer is that you will think so too. I pray that every Christian pastor, elder, deacon, counselor, and church worker reading this book will be challenged by God to join me and others like me in restoring confidence in God's Word as the fundamental textbook for solving life's problems.

---

21   It contains everything necessary to accomplish the task of spiritual restoration.

Presupposition 5

───── Sickness and Sin ─────

I had just finished graduate school and taken my first job working as a biblical counselor in a not-so-biblical counseling center. The telephone rang. A woman on the other end sounded frantic. "Do you make hospital calls?"

"Well, yes, I suppose I do. How can I help you?"

"It's Mickey, my fourteen-year-old son. He's in the psychiatric ward of the local hospital."

"I'm sorry to hear that. What's he in for?"

"We had to commit him because he has been acting strange. He's hearing voices and doing bizarre things—like splattering the walls of his room with some kind of blood-like substance. Will you please go visit him?"

"Sure, what room is he in?"

Up to this point in my life, I had made a fair number of hospital visits. But never had I found it so difficult—never had I had to cut through so much red tape—to get into a patient's room. I learned later that the attending psychiatrist had gone to considerable effort to keep me off the floor (presumably when Mickey's mother told her that I would be stopping by). When I finally got up to the floor, providentially, a young man whom the attending

37

psychiatrist had somehow not yet warned, met me at the door and escorted me directly into Mickey's room.

When I arrived, the patient was eager to see me but was very distressed. Why? Mickey was upset because the hospital staff refused to allow him access to his Bible. Moreover, as he explained to me, they were making fun of (mocking) the fact that he had heard voices. To make matters worse, they were taunting him with the idea that he would have to stay at the funny farm for a very long time. "It's going to take several weeks for us to diagnose your problem, and once we know what's wrong with you, we don't know how long it will take us to treat you," a flock of interns told him.[22]

All this was provided at a cost of $25,000–$30,000 (plus the psychiatrist's fees) per month.[23]

My time with Mickey was cut short (after twenty or thirty minutes) when the psychiatrist entered the room, obviously disturbed that I had made it through her obstacle course. She hastily escorted me to her office.

What happened next has a great deal to do with our fifth presupposition: **Apart from organically caused factors, all of man's voluntary thought and behavior is moral, for which man is responsible before God and neighbor.**

First, the psychiatrist asked me never to come back to see Mickey. (I reluctantly but graciously agreed.) Then, I asked her a crucial question. "Have you ruled out organic (physiological) causes for Mickey's problem?"

"Yes. We're not even going to test anymore."

"Then, what's wrong with him?"

---

22   I don't know for sure, but because Mickey was acting normally, perhaps the hospital staff was trying to evoke another "psychotic episode" by agitating him with their despairing words.

23   Today, the cost for *one day* at a mental health facility would be closer to $3,500. That's over $100,000 per month!

"He's psychotic!"

"Oh, you mean he has a nonorganic illness?"

"Yes, that's right."

At this point, I think she realized my last question was posed to help her see the absurdity of her non-scientific, symptom-based diagnosis, so our conversation came to a rather abrupt halt as I politely said goodbye.

I'll tell you in a moment what eventually happened to Mickey, but for now, let me ask you, What is a nonorganic illness? Either someone is sick, or he isn't. Many "mental health professionals" seem to believe there is some kind of nonorganic "mental germ" that afflicts people who have been diagnosed with most of the 265 "disorders" listed in the DSM-5.[1] Is this so? (Is it scientifically verifiable?)

Thankfully, a growing number of psychiatrists are effectively challenging the American Psychiatric Associations' notion of the disease diagnosis—one based on subjective observations (on a patient's thoughts, feelings, and behavior) without *any* collaborating scientific evidence (lab work). But the DSM-V continues its popularity even though no scientific proof exists that either genetics or chemical imbalances cause most of the syndromes it classifies as diseases.[2] (A syndrome is a cluster of symptoms presumed to be linked.)

The DSM-5 does acknowledge that disorders are syndromes: "A mental disorder is a syndrome characterized by clinically significant disturbances in an individual's cognition, emotional

---

1   Some people argue that the total number is only 157, but there are modifications to some of those that others argue substantially increase the number. But it is not the number of disorders listed in the blue book but rather the symptom-based (behavior-based) rather than organic-based (actual disease) diagnoses mistaken by many as a physiological "mental illnesses" that is most concerning.

2   To be fair, this popularity is probably driven more by the insurance industry than by any other group of "mental health" professionals.

regulation, or behavior that reflects dysfunction in the psychological, biological, or developmental process underlying mental functioning." [3]

Leading psychiatric organizations have acknowledged that they understand neither the causes nor cures of these "mental disorders." They offer theories and opinions (which are often at odds with each other) instead of real medical science. Virtually everything in the affective disorder genre, for example, is *presumed* to be some kind of "chemical imbalance." [4] This, it is said, produces the emotional disturbance (the dysphoria), which can be corrected, for most, by medication. [5]

Of course, the lawyers at the pharmaceutical companies who mass-produce and mass-market this stuff know that the etiological issues of these "mental illnesses" are very iffy. So, they bury the truth in the fine print of the inserts that come with the drugs. Pull down your *Physician Desk Reference* and look for the etiological paragraph (the section that describes how the medication is thought to work), [6] and you will see phrases like "the mechanism of the antidepressant action of . . . 'is presumed to be' or 'is thought to be' or 'is unknown.'" Next time you're online, check out the original Zoloft commercial with those funny little oval critters running around at the bottom of the screen, and listen carefully

---

3 The Diagnostic and Statistical Manual of Mental Disorders, Fifth Edition [italicize] (Arlington, VA, Washington, D.C.: American Psychiatric Association, 2013), 20.

4 Actually, the biogenetic view of the cause of depression has lost popularity in recent years in favor of a newer theory having to do with a portion of the brain called the *amygdala*.

5 But not as many as we have been led to believe. Dr. Charles Hodges, in his excellent, well-documented book, *Good Mood Bad Mood: Help and Hope for Depression and Bipolar Disorder* (Wapwallopen, PA: Shepherd, 2013) demonstrates with scientific research how relatively few people are helped with psychopharmacological treatment.

6 You will find this toward the beginning of each listing under the heading "Clinical Pharmacology."

for the *subjunctive* language used to describe what is *thought* to cause depression. Then, notice how assertively the claim is made that the medication works.

To my knowledge (and I try to stay up on these matters) no tests are currently available to determine the exact chemical status of a person's brain—at least on the brain of a living person.[7] If you doubt this, the next time a counselee tells you he has a chemical imbalance, ask him if he has been shown the lab tests.

"But what about lithium? I know people who get their lithium levels checked regularly!"

The naturally occurring level of lithium carbonate in the human body is either nonexistent or is so minuscule that we don't have the instruments sensitive enough to detect it. Your friends (and counselees) who get tested for lithium do so only *after* they have imbibed a significant amount of the substance for a period of time. The testing is done so the physician can be sure he has not given his patient a toxic dose of this sanity-stabilizing salt.

So, what about this chemical imbalance issue? What if someday scientists find that there really is a chemical imbalance in depressed or anxious people? Would that render the human race no longer responsible? Would it make us morally inculpable for our behavior? Would it nullify the scriptural passages that refer to worry as a sin, or render the unbiblical thoughts associated with depression exempt from God's condemnation? Would it diminish the certainty of such verses as Ecclesiastes 12:14, "For God will bring every act to judgment, everything which is hidden, whether it is good or evil"? It would not. What it *might* do, concerning God's judgment, is to temper it with mercy.[8]

---

7   Much has been made lately about the use of brain scans to substantiate the disease model of mental illness—but looking at colorized pictures of the chemical reactions in one's brain in no way proves a biochemical *origin* for mental illness.

8   God's judgment is perfect. He knows all things. (We know very little, and what we do know, especially of these chemical issues, will almost certainly

We have been fearfully and wonderfully made—largely of chemicals! Every time you stub your toe or sit on a tack, your body generates a chemical and electrical reaction. You have a momentary chemical imbalance. When you get angry, the chemicals in your brain temporarily get out of balance. The question is which came first—the sin or the chemical reaction? If I decide to bang my head against the wall repeatedly, sooner or later, my body chemistry will get out of whack. Now I could take a pill to alleviate the symptoms or, if one were available, to help restore my chemicals to their original pre-head-banging state, or I could simply stop trying to destroy the temple of the Holy Spirit by not banging my head against the wall any longer. In other words, I could stop sinning.

We *are* responsible for our behavior, even when we are tired, ill, or permit sinful thoughts, motives, and actions to so affect the chemicals in our brain that they get out of kilter. Granted, it may be easier to sin and more difficult to obey God in these cases, but where sin abounds, grace super abounds (Rom. 5:20) so that we are without excuse.[9]

---

change in a very short time.) God knows our thoughts from afar, our words before we speak them, and the reasons why we do (or don't) do things. He is the only One who can render judgments about these matters. We know He is merciful, and that He told us, "Mercy triumphs over judgment" (James 2:13). So, if chemical imbalances (and other physiological factors) *not caused by* our own sin are somehow *related to* our sin, God will make (factor in) all the necessary data to judge us perfectly. But again, since we do not yet fully understand the impact of such things on our behavior, we ought to be slow to dogmatically minimize, excuse, justify, or otherwise extenuate behavior that the Bible identifies as sin. Neither should we minimize the impact of physiological factors (such as sleep deprivation, vitamin deficiencies, and real organic illness) on the spiritual condition of those we counsel.

9   The word *grace* in the New Testament does not always mean "unmerited favor." It may also be translated "help." God's help—that is, the supernatural ability and desire that His Spirit provides to those who are in Christ (see Phil. 2:13)—is often what is meant by the word *grace*.

Three Categories of Illness

While visiting Mickey (and his open-minded psychiatrist) in the hospital, I tried to assess what might account for his bizarre behavior. According to the Bible, people become ill due to three causes (or reasons): (1) organic, (2) satanic, and (3) living out of harmony with Scripture. The same three reasons can account for why people do crazy things (why they become "mentally ill"). The first cause is organic. If someone were to sneak up behind me and hit me over the head with a sledgehammer a few times, I would likely develop real mental illness—my thoughts would be discombobulated because my brains would be disassembled. Some people are mentally ill in the truest sense of the word. They suffer from cerebral meningitis, cerebral infections, brain tumors, and the like. When Mickey's psychiatrist (medical doctor) told me she was certain nothing was organically wrong with him, I knew he needed biblical counseling more than medical attention—such as it was. I knew Mickey was dealing with one of the other two causes.

The second source of so-called mental illness is demonic. Some believe that demonic activity still accounts for a number of unregenerate patients in the mental wards of our hospitals.[10] Unpacking this would take an entire book.[11] Suffice it to say that in Scripture, there is evidence that demons influenced people to do bizarre things (see Mark 9:17–18; Luke 9:38–42).

The third and most common reason people act crazy is sin—failing to interpret and live life biblically.

---

10   General editor's note: While believing in the existence of demons, many, because of eschatological reasons, believe demons no longer possess people.

11   Actually, a book I recommend deals with this topic: David Powlison's *Power Encounters: Reclaiming Spiritual Warfare.* It is, at the time of this writing, out of print in print book format but available as an ebook from New Growth Press (https://newgrowthpress.com/ebooks/adult-ebooks/power-encounters-reclaiming-spiritual-warfare-ebook).

Why do you suppose people who habitually practice sinful thinking and sinful behavior manifest symptoms of mental illness? Let me suggest a few reasons.

To begin with, the wages of sin is more sin. The more an individual gives himself over to a particular sin, the more that sin will control him (see John 8:34; Rom. 6:16; 2 Peter 2:19). In time, he will become a slave to that sin, being bound by it. Ultimately, every area of his life will become so affected by the sin that he may even be classified by the biblical name of the sin (liar, thief, angry man, fool, etc.) that has overtaken him (see 1 Cor. 6:9–10).

Second, wrong thoughts, motives (see Heb. 4:12), and actions tend to produce painful emotions that tend to make it easier for us to act irresponsibly. At the risk of oversimplifying a complex series of events, not the least of which is the work of the Holy Spirit through the Word (a process we will cover in a subsequent presupposition), let me ask you to consider the following.

Our internal and external responses (biblical or otherwise) to the circumstances of life generate our emotions. To the extent that we think biblically about providential life events, we will experience emotions that are generally pleasurable (or at least tolerable). If we think unbiblically about what happens, we will likely experience unpleasant emotions. Thoughts and emotions usually affect our actions (good or bad), which in turn, generate additional emotions (pleasant or unpleasant). To the extent that we think and act biblically on a regular basis, we will develop godliness (the character traits of Christ—the fruit of the Spirit). To the extent we habitually think and act unbiblically, we develop ungodliness (character deficiencies and the lusts of the flesh—in increasing measure). So, sinful thinking produces (emotional) misery, which tempts us to respond (act) sinfully. Now, this is the point I want to emphasize. Over a period of time, habitual acts of sin catalyzed by sinful thoughts and unpleasant emotions can manifest themselves in bizarre behavior.

Let's take a simple (and admittedly silly) example. Suppose you go to the office tomorrow and notice that the boss gives you a big smile (*life event*). You tell yourself, "The boss must be pleased with me" (*thought*), so you "feel good" about the smile (*emotion*)— so good, in fact, that you decide to smile right back at him. This *action* generates more pleasant feelings (*emotions*), which cheer you as you do your work.

But now, let's suppose you are in the habit of thinking suspiciously rather than biblically about people ("love . . . believes all things," 1 Cor. 13:7). So, you interpret the smile differently. "That's funny," you *think*. "The boss doesn't usually smile at me. I wonder what's going on. I'm probably in trouble. He's probably smiling at me because he's going to fire me." Then, these suspicious thoughts may begin to generate *feelings* of anxiety and anger. You continue to ruminate (*think*) on them all day until you are so upset *emotionally* that you say to yourself, "He can't fire me; I'll quit." So, you march into his office and angrily tender your resignation (*action*). Now, how do you think you will feel?

A third reason people who habitually sin may end up with bizarre behavior has to do with Proverbs 14:14 (NKJV): "The backslider in heart will be filled with his own ways." If people imagine wild and crazy ways to meet their needs or fulfill their desires, they may soon act out those imaginations in observable behavior.

A fourth possibility to consider is that organically-produced medical problems (real mental illness) may result from sinful behavior. Several days of sleep deprivation, as another example, can produce the same effects as taking LSD: hallucinations. Of course, sleep deprivation is not always the result of personal sin, but it very well could be—as in the case of a college student who is so concerned about acing an exam that she ignores the responsibility she has not to harm her body, the Holy Spirit's temple (1 Cor. 3:16–17, 6:19).

Finally, sometimes, people will act in bizarre ways to get attention or to have some other desire met. Here is a young person who longs inordinately for the attention of others, so she manufactures all manner of symptoms in order to be noticed. (Or perhaps she longs for the buzz that certain medications provide, so she fabricates symptoms to snooker as many doctors as possible into giving her prescriptions.)

As Christians, we believe that "each one of us will give an account of himself to God" (Rom. 14:12). Again, this means that on the day of judgment, no one will be able to hide behind genetic predispositions, unsubstantiated chemical imbalances, DSM labels, or psychosomatic illnesses in an attempt to duck genuine culpability. Now, this doesn't mean that you're going to denigrate, ignore, or even minimize the possible impact of genetics or genuine illness in the life of your counselee. But as a biblical counselor, you would emphasize the grace of God available to him to overcome sin despite the presence of these other factors.

"Okay, I get the idea, but please tell me, what happened to Mickey?"

Well, as it turned out, his mother *was* able to get him out of the hospital in a matter of days and into my office.[12] It took two sessions to get to the root of Mickey's problem: someone in his family had done some very hurtful things to him, and he had responded in bitterness rather than forgiveness. Once he understood his own culpability in the matter, what God expected him to do, and committed himself to a biblical course of action, Mickey's symptoms went away—in a matter of weeks! He couldn't wait to go back to his psychiatrist (at their upcoming checkup session) to show her how much he had improved in such a short period. I was able to dismiss Mickey after several more sessions.

---

12   It should be noted that I didn't instruct her to do this. After realizing that the psychiatrist had stopped looking for organic causes for Mickey's problem, she decided she had no need to employ medical professionals to help her son deal with a nonmedical problem (especially to the tune of $1,000 per day).

I received a call about a year later and learned he was still doing well. He was involved in Bible study and was being discipled by a friend. Still no symptoms. Ten years later, I heard from another friend of his who reported that Mickey had recently gotten married and was doing well (he had had no relapses).

Let me urge you to work hard at developing a close working relationship with physicians in your area who can help you know the extent to which you may be dealing with an organic issue in the life of your counselee. The trick, of course, is finding someone who will do blood work and find genuine pathology.[13] Remember, you are not a physician and should not consider yourself competent in that field. But you are (or should be) competent to counsel the nonorganic problems in the lives of those under your spiritual care.

---

13 This may be especially helpful should you find it necessary to suggest to a counselee that he consider getting a second medical opinion and he asks if you can recommend someone.

Presupposition 6

── Loving God and Loving Neighbor ──

PEOPLE HAVE PROBLEMS with people. Your counselees don't come in saying,

"My car and I aren't getting along."

"My telephone is not speaking to me."

"My teenage refrigerator is rebelling."

"I just can't seem to control my violent bicycle."

Rather, they come in with problems like:

"I can't get along with my boss."

"I'm having a hard time forgiving my husband."

"I don't love my wife anymore."

"I lose my temper with the kids."

"I can't seem to say no to certain temptations."

"I'm depressed, and I worry all the time."

"I feel guilty, lonely, fearful, and despondent."

People are people's problems! People have problems with *persons*:

- They have problems with themselves.

- They have problems with others.
- They have problems with God. (He is a person too.)[1]

Our Lord was asked on one occasion, "Which is the greatest commandment?"

> And one of them, a lawyer, asked Him a question, testing Him, "Teacher, which is the great commandment in the Law?" And He said to him, "You shall love the Lord your God with all your heart, and with all your soul, and with all your mind. This is the great and foremost commandment. The second is like it, You shall love your neighbor as yourself. On these two commandments depend the whole Law and the Prophets." (Matt. 22:35–40)

The fact is, on these two commandments hang the bulk of counseling! Hence, our sixth presupposition: **Every functional behavioral problem that man experiences results from failure to love God or man, or both, as the Bible says he should.**

What is it that you do in the counseling office? You teach people how to love God and how to love others! Can you think of even one problem you have ever faced in your counseling ministry for which the solution could not be boiled down to implementing one or both of these commands? Your job as a biblical counselor is to determine where your counselee is failing to love his God or his neighbor (or both) and to motivate him to implement biblical love.

Think about the breakdown of your counseling cases. If you are like me (and I've been doing this full-time for over thirty-five years with little variation in these basic numbers), 50 percent of your counseling load is marriage counseling, and another 20 to 25 percent is family counseling. Then, there are those interchurch conflicts you are regularly called upon (as a true yokefellow, Phil. 4:3) to resolve. And let's not forget all those in-law problems you've had to help mediate. These problems exist because, at some level, someone does not love his neighbor as himself.

---

1   In a different way, they also have problems with Satan.

And what about the remaining, say, 20 percent or so of your caseload? You know, those "personal problems" like depression, anxiety, and fear for which people come to you, looking for hope and help. Chances are that many, if not most, of those involve broken relationships that require biblical love for one's neighbor (not to mention God) to rectify.[2]

"Ok, I see your point, but how *exactly* does love relate to my counselee's problems?"

Love is the antidote to our greatest problem: the problem of sin.

"I still don't get it. What does love have to do with sin? Connect the dots for me, please."

Practically speaking, what is sin?

"Sin is any want of conformity unto or transgression of the law of God."

No, no, no! That's the theological *definition*. I want you to tell me what the *essence* of sin is *practically*.

"I don't know. But I think I'm going to have a firsthand, practical understanding of what sin is if you don't stop *provoking me to anger* with these silly games you're playing with me."

Okay, here's the deal. I'll spell it out for you and then unpack it piece by piece. The concept of selfishness is, for all intents and purposes, the *practical* equivalent for the concept of sin, and love is the antidote for selfishness.[3]

Now I know that, from a theological perspective, to simply define sin as "selfishness" is incomplete. Any theologically accurate

---

2   In my new position as pastor of counseling at Christ Covenant in Atlanta, GA, where half of the congregation consists of single adults, the statists just mentioned are a bit different: Probably 50 percent of those I see are personal issues, 40 percent marriage and family related, and 10 percent are interpersonal relationship problems.

3   For more on this subject, please see my booklet *Selfishness: From Loving Yourself to Loving Your Neighbor*, from which much of what follows has been extrapolated (Phillipsburg, NJ: P&R, 2010).

understanding of sin ought to include the concept that the transgression is against a holy God. But from a practical (progressive sanctification) perspective, selfishness is probably about as close as you can come to a one-word description.[4]

Sin always involves selfishness. The book of James says, "Each one is tempted when he is carried away and enticed by his own [Gk: *idios*: "pertaining to one's self, one's own, belonging to one's self"] lust. Then when lust has conceived, it gives birth to sin; and when sin is accomplished, it brings forth death" (James 1:14–15).

As Richard Baxter puts it, "Man's fall was his turning from God to himself; and his regeneration consisteth in the turning of him from himself to God. . . . Selfishness is all positive sin in one, as the want of the love of God is all privative [or negative] sin in one."[5] Selfishness is the "mother of all sins." It is the one sin out of which most of the others seem to flow (2 Tim. 3:1–5). To mortify selfishness is to subdue the chief enemy of our souls. It is to remove from the devil the greatest handle by which he attempts to influence and seduce us. Baxter believed that selfishness (love of self) is the quintessence (or epitome) of idolatry:

> I have formerly told you, that self is the god of wicked men, or the worlds greatest idol; And that the inordinate love of pleasure profits and honor, in trinity, is all but this self love in unity. . . . Every man is an idolater, so far as he is selfish. . . . Now selfish ungodly men do all of them rob God, and give His honor and prerogatives to themselves. . . . They call him their God, but will not have Him for . . . their portion . . . nor give Him the strongest love of their

---

4   I would not disagree with those who would argue that the word *disobedience* is another valid one-word practical description of sin, but simply point out that love is *also* the biblical antidote for it. "If you love Me, you will keep [obey] My commandments" (John 14:15; see also 14:21, 23; 15:10; 1 John 5:3; 2 John 6).

5   Richard Baxter, *The Christian Directory* in *The Practical Works of Richard Baxter* (Ligonier, PA: Soli Deo Gloria, 1990), 1:868–869.

hearts: they will not take Him as their absolute owner; and devote themselves and all they have to Him. . . . They will not take Him for their Sovereign, and be ruled by Him, nor deny themselves for Him, nor seek His honor and interest above their own. They call Him their father, but deny Him his honor; and [they call Him] their master, but give Him not His fear. They depend not on His hand, and live not *by* his law, and *to* his glory; and therefore do not take Him for their God. [6]

John Calvin saw it much the same way: "We shall never love our neighbors with sincerity, according to our Lord's intention, until we have corrected the love of ourselves. The two affections are opposite and contradictory."[7]

Because man is sinful (i.e., selfish), God's remedy is for him to learn how to love God and love his neighbor. Hence, the New Testament's emphasis on love has much to do with it being the single best antidote for sin. To put it another way, selfishness is the lack (or opposite) of biblical love.

Let me have your best shot at a one-word definition (synonym) for biblical love. I'll even give you some hints:

- "Walk in love, just as Christ also loved you, and *gave* Himself" (Eph. 5:2).
- "For God so loved the world, that He *gave*" (John 3:16).
- "Husbands, love your wives, just as Christ also loved the church and *gave* Himself" (Eph. 5:25).
- "The life which I now live in the flesh I live by faith in the Son of God, who loved me and *gave* Himself" (Gal. 2:20).

"I get it. Love is giving."

6   Baxter, 1:379.
7   John Calvin, *Commentaries on St. Paul's Epistle to the Galatians and Ephesians* (Grand Rapids: Eerdmans, 1960), .

Right. And selfishness is "taking." But once again, for us to say that "love is giving" without any further qualification would be incomplete.

Let's take a look at the verse that immediately precedes what is arguably the best description of love in the Bible: "And if I *give* all my possessions to feed the poor, and if I surrender [give] my body to be burned, *but do not have love*, it profits me nothing" (1 Cor. 13:3). It is possible to *give* away all your personal possessions and still not have love. And it is possible to make the ultimate sacrifice and *give* up (lay down) your own life and yet not have love.

"What *gives* with you, Lou? First, you argue that love is giving. Then, you prove that giving is not enough."

It's all about motive. Like so many things in the Christian life, what makes something right or wrong is not the action but the attitude of one's heart. Love involves giving without having a selfish primary *motive* for doing so.[8] Selfishness is being more concerned with (interested in or motivated by) what I can get from others than with what I can give them.

> Do not eat the bread of a selfish man,
> Or desire his delicacies;
> For as he thinks within himself, so he is.
> He says to you, "Eat and drink!"
> But his heart is not with you.
> You will vomit up the morsel you have eaten,
> And waste your compliments. (Prov. 23:6–8)

The same principle may, in part, be applied to our love for God. Baxter explains: "Wherever the interest of carnal self is stronger than and more predominant habitually than the interest of God,

---

8   I also like to point out to my counselees the fact that love focuses its attention on the *needs* of others, not necessarily their *wants*. E.g., in Luke 10, Martha apparently thought she *needed* something she really didn't—help in the kitchen. Like her sister, Mary, what she really needed was to sit at the feet of Jesus and hear His words.

of Christ, of everlasting life, there is no true self-denial . . . but where God's interest is the strongest, there self-denial is sincere."[9]

"But isn't that a little simplistic? What about people who have been diagnosed with 'mental disorders'"?

Remember, our presupposition speaks of "functional behavioral problems," not organic ones. Notwithstanding genuine medical factors, the problem with most crazy persons is that they're crazy about themselves. William Kilpatrick, in his book *Psychological Seduction*, explains:

> Extreme forms of mental illness are always extreme cases of self-absorption. . . .
>
> The distinctive quality, the thing that literally sets *paranoid* people apart, is hyper self-consciousness. And the thing they prize most about themselves is *autonomy*. Their constant fear is that someone else is interfering with their will or trying to direct their lives. For this type of person, self-abandonment is the worst fate. Rather than have that happen, they draw deeper into themselves, cutting the cords of sociability as they go.[10]

I would like to give you the final thought on this matter from Richard Baxter. It has to do with the enormity of this problem and the terrible consequences it carries:

> Selfishness is the hardest sin in the world to overcome. In all the unregenerate it is predominant; for nothing but the sanctifying Spirit of God can overcome it. And in many thousands that seem very zealous, in religion and very mortified [self-disciplined], in all other respects, yet in some way or other selfishness doth so lamentably

---

9   Baxter, 1:392.
10   William Kilpatrick, *Psychological Seduction* (Nashville: Thomas Nelson, 1983), 67 (emphasis added).

appear ... and [it] is so strong in many that are sincere, that it is the greatest dishonor to the church of Christ ... and [it] hath tempted many to infidelity, or to doubt whether there be any such thing as true sanctification in the world.[11]

Baxter is saying first that selfishness is predominant in the unsaved, and it is impossible to overcome apart from the sanctifying work of the Holy Spirit—that is, the unregenerate don't have what it takes to overcome their own selfishness.[12] Second, selfishness is present in many zealous and otherwise holy Christians. Third, selfishness is apparent in so many believers who are sincerely following Christ that it disgraces Him and tempts many to remain unconverted.

So, we have our work cut out for us, don't we? Learning to love the Lord and love others is a lifelong task. In fact, it's really what life is all about. Come to think of it, teaching people how to love God and neighbor is what *ministry* (preaching, teaching, and counseling) is all about.

---

11   Baxter, 1:379.
12   Indeed, how can selfishness be put off and love be put on in its place by a person who has not yet had the love of God poured out in his heart (Rom. 5:5; see also 1 John 4:19)?

Presupposition 7

——— COUNSELING AND REGENERATION ———

THERE SEEMS TO BE A bit of confusion these days in Christian circles about who's running and powering the ship. A variety of theologies abound as to the exact role of the Holy Spirit in the sanctification process. This confusion is no small issue in the arena of "Christian counseling."

One term in particular is often *misapplied* by some who are *misinformed* about biblical counseling. Like the Sadducees who did not believe in a bodily resurrection, they seem to understand neither the Scriptures nor the power of God. The term I often hear misapplied is the phrase "in the flesh."

"You biblical counselors are just religious behavior modification specialists: you teach people how to change *in the flesh.*"

Or, on the other side of the spectrum, "If those you counsel do anything to change themselves before they are led by the Spirit to do so, they'll just be doing it *in the flesh!*"

What these well-meaning and sincere but oft-misguided people mean by the term "in the flesh" is some sort of *self-initi-ated, carnal* effort on the part of the Christian that is intended to produce changes in his life without dependence on the Spirit of God. While I agree with the sentiment of this argument—that Christians cannot change in ways that please God apart from

God's grace and that self-effort without dependence on Him will not produce such change—there is *no place* in Scripture where the term "in the flesh" is used this way. More importantly, the Bible specifically teaches that this phrase *doesn't* apply to believers at all: "However, *you are not in the flesh* but in the Spirit, if indeed the Spirit of God dwells in you. But if anyone does not have the Spirit of Christ, he does not belong to Him" (Rom. 8:9).

In his first book, *Competent to Counsel,* Jay Adams addresses the underlying assumption and presupposition that Christians must depend on the Holy Spirit's power for their personal and progressive sanctification:

> Frequent references to the place of the Holy Spirit in counseling will be made specifically throughout this book, but wherever his work has not been spelled out in detail, it is *everywhere assumed.* Since concrete methodology in counseling will often be discussed at length, it might be possible to dip into portions of the book and get the impression that the Holy Spirit has been supplanted by human techniques. But I it precisely this disjunction which is false. When the Holy Spirit *moved directly in the hearts* of believers in Jerusalem to motivate them by love to pool their goods for the sake of the poor, He was no more at work than when Paul *organized and conducted* a successful fundraising campaign throughout the Mediterranean world for the same purpose.

> It is perfectly lawful, and often necessary for the believer to initiate a course of action based on the Word of God to accomplish a Biblical goal with the *assumption* that the Holy Spirit will *bless the plan* and *empower the saint* to accomplish that goal.

> Methodology and technique, skill and the exercise of gifts are all consonant with the work of the Spirit. What makes the difference is one's attitude and inner motivation: does he do what he does in reliance upon his own efforts, in

dependence upon methods and techniques, or does he acknowledge his own inability and ask the Spirit to use his gifts and methods? Gifts, methodology and technique, of course, may be abused; they may be set over against the Spirit and may be used to replace his work. But they also may be used in complete subjection to him to the glory of God and the benefit of his children.

Then, citing W. T. Davidson's book *The Indwelling Spirit*, he concludes,

> Davison has well stated this point when he rightly warns against the attempt to secure a spiritual end by the adoption of habits, the multiplication of rules, and the observance of external standards, excellent in themselves, but useful only as means subordinate to the Spirit.[13]

Our *seventh* presupposition is as follows: **Regeneration by the Holy Spirit is a prerequisite for biblical change and obedience on the part of the counselee.**

The goal of *all* counseling is change. This is perhaps the only thing the three hundred-plus current theories of psychotherapy have in common. Indeed, the hope of helping people change is, at some level, what motivates counselors to counsel. But a person can only change in two ways: *inwardly* or *outwardly*. Biblical counseling hopes to effect a change in the heart of the counselee. And allow me to say it again, only a change at that level of depth can please God.

"But what about secular counselors who do cognitive counseling? Don't they deal with heart issues?"

They may well deal with thoughts (less so with motives), but their understanding of these things is far from biblical.[14] They

---

13   Jay E. Adams, *Competent to Counsel* (Grand Rapids: Zondervan, 2009), 24–25.

14   Even some non-cognitive models may claim to deal with motives. E.g., Freudian therapists attempt to discover *unconscious drives* that they believe are hidden from the patient. The therapy comes not so much from *changing* these drives but in *bringing them to the surface* (conscious). This insight-oriented

simply do not have the proper "diagnostic manual" to identify thought problems from God's point of view (see Heb. 12:4). And without the Spirit of God applying the Word of God in sanctifying power to the mind and will of the counselee, even an accurate understanding of the problem does little good.

An unsaved counselee may be able to *reform* his life to a certain degree and perhaps *conform* to his self-imposed standards (or those of his therapist). But what he cannot do without the Holy Spirit is *transform* himself into the image of Christ. What's more, the changes he is able to make "in the flesh" do not please God. "Those who are in the flesh [unbelievers] cannot please God" (Rom. 8:8).

Moreover, the Bible is necessary to diagnose and correct the deeper issues of the heart, for the Word of God is the discerner of the thoughts and intents of the heart (Heb. 4:12). The Spirit uses the Word (His sword) to bring about change. To expect an unregenerate counselee to truly understand, let alone consistently apply, the Bible is not only foolish, it is patently unbiblical because "a natural man does not accept the things of the Spirit of God, for they are foolishness to him; and he cannot understand them, because they are spiritually appraised" (1 Cor. 2:14; see also John 3:19–21).

In that very place, at this very moment, wherever you happen to be reading this book, there are hundreds (perhaps thousands) of voices all around you. But unless you have the right equipment (FM, AM, shortwave, police band radios, telephones, and satellite receivers), you can't hear them. Likewise, the unbeliever doesn't have the equipment to hear and decipher God's Spirit speaking to him in the Holy Scriptures.

Now, what implications does this presupposition have on counseling unbelievers? I will only mention three.

---

approach supposedly produces a life-changing catharsis for the one being counseled. The concept of pleasing God by repenting of wrong motives is anathema to this system.

First, since a counselor's ability to successfully counsel (or change) an unbeliever will be severely limited until the counselee is saved, the way you counsel an unbeliever will be quite different from how you counsel a believer. As Jay Adams puts it, "You can't counsel an unbeliever in the full biblical sense of that word *counsel*."[15] It's not that you are going to ignore his concerns and not do anything to help him understand his problems biblically[16] or do little else but preach the gospel to him until he believes.[17]

Second, the gospel should be proclaimed to the counselee as soon as possible. It's not that you will tell the unsaved counselee not to return until he is ready to trust Christ (at least not initially), but since you do not know how many more times your paths will meet, you cannot presume you can get to the gospel "several sessions later." I make it my practice if I don't *thoroughly* present the gospel in the first session (which, incidentally, I find I am seldom able to do) to give the counselee something for homework that has the gospel spelled out clearly. (I am especially fond of Jay Adams's "What to Do When" pamphlets as well as several full-color booklets published by Evangelical Press.)[18]

---

15   Jay Adams, appendix A, "What to Do When You Counsel an Unbeliever," in *A Theology of Christian Counseling*, Grand Rapids: Zondervan,), 320.

16   Quite the contrary, in fact. Time and time again, when I have helped unbelievers diagnose their problems in biblical terms, it has offered them hope. This has been largely due to the fact that (1) an accurate biblical diagnosis is often so refreshingly different than what they have been told in the past, and because (2) a biblical diagnosis lacks the obfuscated psychobabble that is not only illogical but often requires equally unbiblical constructs to be learned to find solutions, and (3) a biblical diagnosis eschews the hopelessness of some secular diagnoses when they imply that the counselee is totally a victim and therefore is not in a position to do much about the problem.

17   Indeed, if you violate Prov. 18:2, 17 by not listening carefully, compassionately, and completely, without taking his concerns seriously, you may actually make it harder for him to hear the gospel. Don't be in too much of a rush! Remember you can always send him home with an assignment that will expose him to the gospel.

18   I have recently written a booklet entitled *Biblical Counseling: What to Expect* (Kress, 2017) that discloses to my new counselees the importance of

Third, all counseling (or precounseling) should revolve around leading the counselee to Christ. Since the counseling you do with unsaved individuals is essentially problem-oriented evangelism, it is essential to be upfront (honest) with your counselees who do not profess Christ about your limited ability to help them apart from the Holy Spirit quickening them. The point I want my unregenerate counselees to get as soon as possible is this: "God has answers to all the problems you have told me about, but you can't have (access to) them until you become a Christian."[19]

Let me conclude this chapter with another quote from Jay Adams. And please don't forget to read the appendix to pick up some practical tips on "how to do problem-oriented evangelism."

> Jesus helped many people, sometimes with superficial problems on a superficial basis first, but always in connection with evangelism. When healing bodies, for example, he always connected the greater healing of the eyes of the *heart* or the paralysis of the *heart* or the leprosy of the *heart* with the physical healing. That's just what you must do in counseling. You must approach unbelievers with both hands. You have something in both hands to offer: in one hand something very minimal, and in the other the entrance into real counseling, change at a level of depth that begins with the Gospel of the Lord Jesus Christ.[20]

---

the gospel to the counseling process. Under the heading "You should expect to hear much (and learn much) about Jesus Christ," I explain, "Your counselor may, by various means, try to help you determine if you truly have been born again—especially if he has any doubts. If he does have such doubts he will urge you to make your calling and election sure' (cf. 2 Peter 1:4–10)."

19   Obviously, this point can (and in most cases, *should*) be made more thoroughly and graciously than I have stated it, but it is the message they need to hear.

20   Adams, "What to Do When You Counsel an Unbeliever," 320–321.

Presupposition 8

———— The Spirit and the Word ————

THERE IS NO SUCH THING as instant spiritual growth—at least not in this life. There is no pill you can give them, no class to which you can send them, no homework you can assign them, no whiffle dust you can sprinkle over them that will quickly transform those you counsel into the image of Christ and bring them to maturity. Maturity takes time.

The term *progressive sanctification* is so called because it occurs continuously throughout our lives rather than instantaneously. The Holy Spirit is the Principal Agent who sanctifies, working in the hearts of all true believers to make them more like Christ. But He does so by means of the Word.

This brings us to our eighth presupposition: **The only behavioral changes in man that are pleasing to God and are ultimately beneficial to man are those effected by means of the Holy Spirit applying the Word of God in sanctifying power to the will and mind of the counselee in accordance with biblical methods and directives.**

A person simply cannot change in ways pleasing to God apart from the Spirit working in conjunction with the Word. The Holy Spirit must have His most effective weapon (the sword of the Spirit) if He is to so change you and your believing counselees.

Like regeneration, sanctification is an act of God.[1] But unlike regeneration, it is an act of God that requires our cooperation.[2] The single most important way you and I can cooperate with Him is by getting His Word into our hearts. As a counselor, you must cooperate with His work in your counselee's life by motivating him to let Christ's word richly dwell in his heart (Col. 3:16).

An astounding number of Christians believe they can grow in grace apart from regular and continuous time in the Word (i.e., Bible reading, study, memorization, meditation, and active listening to Bible preaching and teaching). At the risk of overstating my argument, let me say it this way: It doesn't matter how much praying or fasting or "fellowshipping" with other Christians or ministering or witnessing to others you may do; if you're not spending time in God's Word (or to be more accurate, if God's Word does not richly dwell in you), you are limiting the Holy Spirit's sanctifying influence in your life. Oh, it is not that He is unable to work if we don't cooperate. It's that He has not promised to work apart from the Bible.

> That the Holy Spirit operates through the Bible is . . . confirmed in that what the Bible is said to do, the Spirit is likewise said to do. For example, each of the four functions of Scripture (listed below) is said to be performed also by the Holy Spirit (in the verses added):
>
> 1. "Teaching": compare 1 John 2:27 (the "anointing" represents the Holy Spirit).
>
> 2. "Conviction": compare John 16:7–11.
>
> 3. "Correction": compare Galatians 6:1; 5:22, 23.

---

1   Regeneration is the instantaneous change in man's governing disposition (nature) that occurs as the Spirit of God gives new life to those who truly believe in Jesus Christ.

2   Being dead in our trespasses and sins, we do not have the ability to cooperate until the Holy Spirit quickens us.

4. "Disciplined training in righteousness": compare
Galatians 5:16–18; Romans 6–8.

In each case, the Spirit works by means of the Bible."[3]

A further indication of the Spirit's working by means of the Word can be seen by comparing the language of two parallel passages of Scripture.

But first, may I ask you a rather personal question?[4] Are you Spirit-filled? At this very moment, as you are sitting there reading this book, can you honestly say you are filled with the Spirit?

"I'm in the ministry! Of course I'm filled with the Spirit! (Well, I am most of the time anyway)."

Good. But how did you get that way? Exactly how does one become filled with the Spirit?

In Ephesians 5:18, we are commanded, "Do not get drunk with wine, for that is dissipation [that will lead to the disintegration of your life], but be filled with the Spirit." This verse is followed by a series of general instructions and directives addressed to specific individuals. These instructions and directives flow out of the initial command to be Spirit-filled. These same directions can be found almost verbatim in the book of Colossians (3:16–25) where they are not associated with the Spirit but with the Word. "Let the word of Christ richly dwell within you." (The following chart will help you do your own verse-by-verse analysis of these two passages.) In addition to demonstrating the close relationship between the Spirit and the Word, the similarity between these two passages also provides insight into the means whereby He fills us. To the degree that a person allows the Word of God to fill his heart, the Spirit fills his life.

---

3   Jay Adams, *How to Help People Change* (Grand Rapids, Ministry Resources Library, 1986).

4   Asking this question, "May I ask you a rather personal question?" (asking permission before intruding) can be an effective way to initiate a line of questioning that might otherwise make a counselee squirm.

Ephesians	Colossians
5:18 "Be filled with the Spirit."	**3:16** "Let the word of Christ richly dwell within you."
5:19–20 "Speaking to one another in psalms and hymns and spiritual songs, singing and making melody with your heart to the Lord; always giving thanks for all things in the name of our Lord Jesus Christ to God, even the Father."	**3:16–17** "teaching and admonishing one another with psalms and hymns and spiritual songs, singing with thankfulness in your hearts to God." And whatever you do in word or deed, do all in the name of the Lord Jesus, giving thanks through Him to God the Father.
5:22 "Wives, be subject to your own husbands, as to the Lord."	**3:18** "Wives, be subject to your husbands, as is fitting in the Lord."
5:25 "Husbands, love your wives, just as Christ also loved the church and gave Himself up for her."	**3:19** "Husbands, love your wives, and do not be embittered against them."
6:1 "Children, obey your parents in the Lord, for this is right."	**3:20** "Children, be obedient to your parents in all things, for this is well-pleasing to the Lord."
6:4 "And fathers, do not provoke your children to anger; but bring them up in the discipline and instruction of the Lord."	**3:21** "Fathers, do not exasperate your children, that they may not lose heart."

6:5–8 "Slaves, be obedient to those who are your masters according to the flesh, with fear and trembling, in the sincerity of your heart, as to Christ; not by way of eyeservice, as men-pleasers, but as slaves of Christ, doing the will of God from the heart. With good will render service, as to the Lord, and not to men, knowing that whatever good thing each one does, this he will receive back from the Lord, whether slave or free."	**3:22–24** "Slaves, in all things obey those who are your masters on earth, not with external service, as those who [merely] please men, but with sincerity of heart, fearing the Lord. Whatever you do, do your work heartily, as for the Lord rather than for men; knowing that from the Lord you will receive the reward of the inheritance. It is the Lord Christ whom you serve."
6:9 "And, masters, do the same things to them, and give up threatening, knowing that both their Master and yours is in heaven, and there is no partiality with Him."	**4:1** "Masters, grant to your slaves justice and fairness, knowing that you too have a Master in heaven."

So, if you want your counselees to be sanctified and Spirit-filled, you will often have to invest some time in training them to find and internalize those specific Scripture passages appropriate to their counseling issues. Remember, the Spirit's fruit does not grow overnight but gradually develops as it is nourished with the Word of God.

Zap Theology: The Kiss-and-Make-Up-with-God Syndrome

"Pastor, I've been struggling with this sin for seven years and can't seem to get it under control."

"I'm glad you came to see me about this. Tell me, what exactly have you done as you have 'struggled.'"

"Well, let's see. I have prayed about it. I have confessed it to the Lord and asked for forgiveness a hundred times. I have told Him how sorry I am that I keep falling into it. I have asked Him to help me not to do it anymore. I have even made a vow not to do it again—which I only kept for thirteen days.

"Did you find someone to hold you accountable?"

"Not really."

"Did you radically amputate those things in your life regularly causing you to stumble?"

"Well, sort of, but I didn't get rid of everything."

"I see. Have you found those passages in the Bible that deal with this particular sin, internalized them, and meditated on them day and night?"

"Well, I guess I looked at a few of them, but I didn't break open my concordance if that's what you mean."

"Well, tell me, how often do you read your Bible?"

"Oh, I'd say on an average of two or three times a week."

"How do you expect the Holy Spirit to change you if you are not fully cooperating with Him?"

"I guess I've just been kidding myself into thinking I was doing everything I could to solve my problem."

"Would it be more accurate to say that you have been deceiving yourself into thinking that the Lord was going to change you without your having to do your part—that the Lord was going make some kind of special exception when it comes to your sanctification?"

Many Christians don't really struggle at all when they "struggle" with sin. Instead, they confess their sin to God, pray that He will help them change, and promptly get off their knees expecting (believing) that God has somehow infused ("zapped") them with a special measure of grace that will enable them to never commit the same sin again, without any (or very little) further effort on their part. This is what is sometimes referred to as "the kiss-and-make-up-with-God syndrome."

It is not enough merely to pray that God will change us. We must also *do* what the Bible says is necessary to "put off" the sin and "put on" Christ. Change is a twofold process for the Christian. We actually put off our sin by putting on its biblical antithesis. Put another way, Christians don't "break" habits—pagans do. Christians replace bad habits with good ones.

It is not enough for the Christian who habitually lies to simply stop lying. He must make it his goal to become truthful. "Therefore, laying aside falsehood, speak truth each one of you with his neighbor, for we are members of one another" (Eph. 4:25). It is not enough for a thief to just stop stealing. He must not only put off *stealing* but also put on *diligence* and *generosity.* "He who steals must steal no longer; but rather he must labor, performing with his own hands what is good, so that he will have something to share with the one who has need" (Eph. 4:28).

This "put off/put on" dynamic can only happen as the mind is renewed through the Scriptures. As our presupposition states, the changes wrought by the Holy Spirit "are effected by means of the Holy Spirit applying the Word of God in sanctifying power to the will and mind of the counselee."

> That, in reference to your former manner of life, you *lay aside* the old self, which is being corrupted in accordance with the lusts of deceit, *and that you be renewed in the spirit of your mind*, and *put on* the new self, which in the likeness of God has been created in righteousness and holiness of the truth. (Eph. 4:22–24)

> And do not be conformed to this world, but be trans-
> formed by the *renewing of your mind*, that you may prove
> what the will of God is, that which is good and acceptable
> and perfect. (Rom. 12:2)

The Holy Spirit takes the Scriptures you have opened to your
believing counselee and have urged him to internalize (through
Bible reading, study, memorization, meditation, etc.) and changes
(transforms) him from the inside. Since those you counsel cannot
properly be sanctified apart from God's Word—since the Word
of God is necessary to produce lasting change in the lives of your
believing counselees—your job is to convince him of his need to
marinate his mind in the relevant Scriptures.

The last section of our presupposition excludes all unbiblical methods of change that are not "in accordance with biblical
methods and directives." A biblical counseling model reflects the
Scriptures *at every point* (major and minor). For every bit of advice
you give your counselees, you must be sure you have solid biblical
support. At any point in the process, they have the right to stop
you and ask you to explain the biblical basis for your counsel.
(Of course, you should make every effort to explain the theology
behind the directions you give *before* you are asked.) It's not that
everything you tell them must be based on a biblical directive
(imperative, command), but there ought to be a firm biblical principle behind everything you say. Moreover, there is often more
than one way to skin a cat, biblically speaking. Sometimes, I say
to my counselees, when I give advice based on a biblical principle
rather than a directive, something like this: "Unless you have a
better idea (in other words, unless you can come up with another
biblically derived solution), I strongly suggest that you do this."

Jay Adams taught me years ago to distinguish between biblically directed solutions and biblically derived solutions to problems. Sometimes, the answer to a problem is clearly delineated
in the Bible. That is, in order to solve the problem, specific scriptural commands must be obeyed. In cases like this, the biblically

directed solution will usually involve teaching your counselee about those passages that command him to take action (if he is not already familiar with them) and helping him devise a plan to implement them.[5] The Bible is filled with directed counsel for very specific kinds of problems. Additionally, there is a plethora of scriptural commands that, if not followed, will engender God's displeasure and produce painful consequences. Sometimes, the solution to life's problems is found by simply beginning to obey certain clear biblical directives.

Sometimes, the solution to a particular problem is not delineated in the Scriptures and must therefore be derived from appropriate biblical principles. These are what we like to call *biblically derived solutions*. A biblically derived solution is devised in accordance with biblical principles by the Christian to accomplish a biblical goal for which no specific directives are given in Scripture.[6]

Suppose, for example, one of the men in your church loses his job. Initially, he handles it well. But after several weeks of being unable to find work, he goes from being discouraged to being filled with self-pity to being depressed. His wife convinces him to come to you for counseling. Your job, among other things, is to help him develop a plan for gainful employment. After all, the Bible does say in 2 Thessalonians 3:10, "If anyone is not willing to work, then he is not to eat, either."

"But, isn't that a directive?"

It is. "To eat" is a present active imperative. So, do you tell the counselee, "You are living in sin as long as you are unemployed— get a job!"?

---

5   Jay Adams, in *What to Do on Thursday* (an INS publication), refers to these as "biblically directed methods" (Hackettstown, NJ: Timeless Texts, 1995), 105.
6   See *What to Do on Thursday*, 105–110, for Adam's discussion of the validity and use of both *biblically directed* and *biblically derived* methods of implementing passages of Scripture.

"No, it's not that simple. Besides, the Bible doesn't say he must have a paying job—it says he must work!"

Exactly! But he is discouraged and depressed. So, you must help him come up with a plan based on the biblical goal of working for his food. The Bible says he must work (the biblical goal), but it doesn't give him specific instructions on how to find a job.

Now, you must turn to other passages to help you put together a biblically based plan to help him find work. Here is what such a plan might entail.

My Plan for Finding Employment

Biblically Derived Activity	Scripture on Which Activity Is Based
I will spend at least ten minutes each day praying daily for a new job.	Matthew 6:11: "Give us this day our daily bread." James 4:2: "You do not have because you do not ask."
I will spend at least thirty hours each week looking for gainful employment. (After all, I really do have a job—finding one.)	2 Thessalonians 3:10–12: "For even when we were with you, we used to give you this order: if anyone is not willing to work, then he is not to eat, either. For we hear that some among you are leading an undisciplined life, doing no work at all, but acting like busybodies. Now such persons we command and exhort in the Lord Jesus Christ to work in quiet fashion and eat their own bread."

I will keep track on an index card (or time-tracker app) not only of the hours I spend looking for work each day but also of the specific things I do to find work (making phone calls, working on and sending out my resume, going on interviews, etc.).	Ephesians 5:15–17: "Therefore be careful how you walk, not as unwise men but as wise, making the most of your time, because the days are evil. So then do not be foolish, but understand what the will of the Lord is." Luke 16:10: "He who is faithful in a very little thing is faithful also in much; and he who is unrighteous in a very little thing is unrighteous also in much." (See also vv. 1–8.)
I will make a list of the people at church who may be able to directly or indirectly help me find work. I will begin to interview each one willing to meet with me.	Proverbs 27:10: "Do not go to your brother's house in the day of your calamity; better is a neighbor who is near than a brother far away." James 2:15–16: "If a brother or sister is without clothing and in need of daily food, and one of you says to them, 'Go in peace, be warmed and be filled,' and yet you do not give them what is necessary for their body, what use is that?"

I will also spend ten hours each week looking for a short-term, part-time job to help me make ends meet.	Ecclesiastes 11:6: "Sow your seed in the morning and do not be idle in the evening, for you do not know whether morning or evening sowing will succeed, or whether both of them alike will be good."
I will remind myself every evening that even though I don't have a job yet, I can eat my supper with gladness of heart, knowing that I have put in a good day's work.	Ecclesiastes 2:24: "There is nothing better for a man than to eat and drink and tell himself that his labor is good. This also I have seen that it is from the hand of God."

Usually, both biblically directed solutions and biblically derived solutions are necessary to solve problems effectively.

Let me give you one final word of caution: a *biblically derived* solution must never be elevated to the place of a *biblically directed* one. To not distinguish between the two by raising a biblical *principle* to the level of a *command* is to run the risk of being legalistic. Imagine how you might respond if you were the one who had lost his job and your counselor told you you were biblically obligated to fulfill each activity in the chart above "to the letter."

What are the practical implications of this presupposition for you as a counselor? Let me give you three. First, your counselees must be taught the importance of regular (daily) Bible reading and study. (Usually, the first commitment I ask my counselees to make in the initial session is to "spend a minimum of ten minutes each day reading the Bible for at least as long as you are in counseling.")[7] Second, above and beyond this, specific portions of relevant Scripture passages should be assigned for your counselees to internalize. Third, you cannot change behavior apart from changing cognition—you cannot change how your counselee acts without teaching him to change how he thinks (see Rom. 12:2; Eph. 4:23).

Changing people's minds and changing their behavior (changing the direction of their lives) is essentially what counseling (and what the word "repentance") is really all about.[8] We can efficaciously do neither without the Spirit or His Sword! May we learn to increasingly depend upon them as we seek to sanctify ourselves and those to whom we minister.

---

7   Of course, if necessary, I will give them instruction on how to do this (if not specific Bible studies tailored to solving their particular problems). Don't forget to consider other homework assignments such as books, audio recordings, podcasts, pamphlets, etc. that can be assigned regularly. And be sure your counselee is faithfully attending worship services at a Bible-believing church, as sitting under the preaching of God's Word is an essential means of Scripture intake.

8   The Old Testament word for *repentance* is *shuv* ("to turn around"); the New Testament word is *metanoieo* ("to rethink, change the mind"). Combining the two gives a full understanding of repentance. Jay E. Adams, *The Practical Encyclopedia of Christian Counseling* (Hackettstown, NJ: Timeless Texts, 2003).

Presupposition 9

———— Principles and Practices ————

THE PRESUPPOSITION WE will consider next is the most controversial of the lot. It is, for many, a watershed mark—the point at which those who heartily agree with all the previous presuppositions often stumble. Yet it is *the* one foundational truth that, more than any other, characterizes the historic biblical counseling movement.[1] Presupposition 9: **All methodology must grow out of biblical principles and practices (thus, non-Christian content or methods have no place in biblical counseling).**

Most counselors who are Christians are eclectic in their approach to helping people change. That is, they "call out and gather together" from the many secular theories of psychology, principles, and practices to supplement biblical truth. Why? Although they believe in the verbal, plenary inspiration of Scripture, they deny its sufficiency. Oh, to be sure, some of them would balk at the suggestion that they do not believe the Scripture to be totally sufficient "for life and godliness" (1 Peter 1:3). But there

---

1 That is, this presupposition characterizes the original "nouthetic" biblical counseling movement—not one of the growing numbers of so-called biblical counseling imitations that deny this presupposition. Indeed, to deny the sufficiency of Scripture is to forfeit the right to call one's theory (or, as we shall see, theology) of counseling "biblical."

is no escaping the reality that, in practice, to the degree they are supplementing what the Bible has to say about changing people with principles and practices found elsewhere, they view the Scriptures as inadequate. *Integration* is their buzzword, and "all truth is God's truth" is their mantra.

The crux of the matter is the extent to which Christian counselors should incorporate secular *methods of change* (not found in Scripture) into their counseling model.

Before we go further, we should remind ourselves of something we looked at in a previous presupposition: the distinction between two kinds of secular psychology: descriptive psychology, which is not necessarily competitive to biblical counseling, and clinical (or counseling) psychology, which necessarily is. The first involves the study of the soul; the second involves its cure. The first merely *describes* human behavior; the second *prescribes* its therapy. The first seeks to recognize human behavior; the last seeks to remedy it.

As you may remember, I have already maintained that describing human behavior does not necessarily compete with the Bible because the Bible does not claim to be a book that describes every aspect of every human behavior.[2] It does not, for example, explain at what approximate age children's thought patterns change from basically concrete to more abstract in nature. Neither does it explain all the apparent differences between the sexes. In this regard, then, the Bible is not, strictly speaking, a textbook for psychology.

> Although the Bible has much to say concerning human behavior, it has not been given primarily for that purpose. Since it does address this issue, however, it ought to be the *first* book consulted by Christian descriptive psychologists so that biblical terminology can be employed to describe those behaviors that are defined in Scripture "not

---

2   It describes human behavior sufficiently to help us make a biblical diagnosis of all nonorganic problems resulting from sin.

with the words that man's wisdom teaches, but that which the Holy Spirit teaches."[3]

But what about counseling or clinical psychology—is it ever necessary, or even helpful, to supplement what the Bible says with so-called truth from secular counseling therapies? While it is true that the Bible makes no claims to function exclusively as a systematic, all-inclusive taxonomy of human behavior (as has also been established in presupposition 4), it does repeatedly claim to function as a fully sufficient counseling textbook.

Historic biblical counseling, therefore, opposes the practice of integrating theology (the theology of how man is to be transformed into the image of Christ) with secular psychology. Webster's dictionary defines *integration* as "to form, coordinate or blend into a functioning or unified whole."[4] The idea is that when integrated, two entities are blended together in such a way as to form a new and complete (whole) entity.[5] The clear implication of this "blend" is that both entities are *insufficient* to do the job that the new one was created to do.

Various models have been postulated to describe (and even diagram) how such an integration might work. The bottom line

---

3   Originally published in *The Journal of Modern Ministry*, volume 2, number 1, p. 65.

4   *Webster's Collegiate Dictionary*, 15th ed. (1979), s.v. "integration." (For years, Christian eclectic counselors have been trying to produce a "unified whole" model of counseling by blending psychology and theology. Yet today the search for the "perfect" integration model goes on. The description on the cover of *The Journal of Psychology and Theology*, published by Biola University for almost fifty years, reveals that integration is the purpose of this publication: "An Evangelical Forum for the Integration of Psychology and Theology."

5   Carter and Narramore, e.g., in *The Integration of Theology and Psychology* explain, "The truths of psychology are not contradictory to the truths of divine revelation; in fact, they have the potential of being *integrated* into a *harmonious whole*." John Carter and Bruce Narramore, *The Integration of Theology and Psychology* (Grand Rapids: Zondervan, 1980), 49, emphasis added.

for all of them, however, is that there are bits of truth somehow necessary for man's progressive sanctification that God has not given us in special revelation but are available only through general revelation. The proponents of integration may balk (or even croak) that I would express their view in this way, but I have yet to hear anyone convincingly deny that this is what integrationists believe.

(Now, before I go any further, may I say with all sincerity and as much humility as I can muster that most integrationists I know are very warm, sincere, committed Christians who love Christ. I am convinced some have progressed further in their sanctification than I have.[6] My issue is not with them personally. It is simply a matter of what they believe and teach versus what the Bible says.)

"It may not need much," they reason, "it may not always be necessary, but the Bible simply *doesn't* have what it takes to help all believers solve all of life's (nonorganic) personal problems. So, we must look to psychology for supplementation."

This opens the door for them to incorporate unbiblical content into their model (theology) of counseling.

The practice of integration is usually justified by the belief that the "truth" found outside Scripture (general revelation) is on the same level as truth found within the Scriptures. The integrationist motto is "All truth is God's truth."

This slogan insinuates that the so-called truth outside the Bible is just as valid as the truth in the Bible. But there are at least two essential differences between the truth of Scripture and the "truth" derived from non-biblical sources. First, the data found in the Bible is *divinely inspired*. It is absolutely and positively without question the truth (John 17:17), while all such non-biblical data lacks divine authority.

Moreover, the data found in the Bible is *eternal* truth, while all such data derived from non-biblical sources is neither impeccable

---

6   And I suspect they would have progressed even further had their devotion to psychology not slowed them down.

nor necessarily eternal truth---at least in the form we now perceive it to be. The very concept of integration suggests that "truth"
revealed outside of Scripture will stand forever unchanged and
unchallenged, even though scientific data is frequently being
revised with each passing day.[7] How much more will today's scientific data be susceptible to change (or, at least, to fine-tuning)
when we receive our glorified bodies?

Jay Adams makes the point that to determine what truth is,
a compressive knowledge of certain essential things is necessary.

> God's knowledge is comprehensive. He knows all things.
> And, He knows each of them in relation to all other
> things. Man's grasp on Truth—though in part commu-
> nicated to him by God—can never be comprehensive. He
> can neither know all things nor how all things relate to
> one another. How, then, can man really know the Truth?
>
> The problem is this: since God's Truth has arisen from
> His comprehensive knowledge of all things, how can man
> ever be sure that he has Truth? Surely, he doesn't possess
> such vast knowledge. Yet without it, what seems to him to
> be true might no longer be so viewed if he were in posses-
> sion of more pieces of the whole in their proper relations
> toward all other things, as God is. He might see things
> quite differently. Indeed, he might declare what he previ-
> ously thought true, "false."[8]

Think of gravity. Are you really sure that when we get to
heaven, the equation currently used to formulate the attraction
between two bodies won't be revised? And what can be said about

---

7 Ironically, this is especially the case in the realm of psychiatry where the
   psychotropic cocktails for the treatment of various "psychiatric disorders"
   seemingly changes every quarter as medical journals compete to publish the
   "latest research findings."
8 Jay E. Adams, *Is All Truth God's Truth?* (Stanley, NC: Timeless Texts,
   2003), 3–4. I have included the entire chapter on the "Insufficiency of General Revelation," in the appendix.

the science of nutrition? You may be old enough to remember when the "state of the art" formula for nutrition was expressed not in terms of a pyramid (a triangle with much greater allowances for certain foods at the base than at the apex) as it is today but a square with four equal categories of "food groups."[9] Consider also the US government Body Mass Index (weight for height) guidelines, which were recently revised.

The fallacy with the statement, "All truth is God's truth," is not that all truth is not true but that all the non-biblical data we now possess is 100 percent absolute eternal truth. The only truth that is 100 percent absolute eternal truth, which will never be changed, altered, or improved on, is the Word of God. To try to "blend" absolute eternal truth with uninspired temporal truth to create a "unified whole" is as futile as trying to homogenize oil and vinegar with a teaspoon—it may appear to work for a while, but in time, it will separate.

"But," you say, "how can the integration of psychology and theology be wrong if Christians in other fields integrate theology with their particular field of study? Don't mathematicians, scientists, and musicians integrate the Bible with their disciplines? What's the difference?"

The Bible never claims to be a textbook for math, science, or music. So that argument is a moot point. The Bible is not a book specifically written as a textbook for those purposes but rather (among other things) to provide the answers for man's behavioral problems and the means for man's behavioral changes. There is no need to scrounge around the psychiatrist's table hoping to find some morsel of sanctifying truth the Holy Spirit left out of Scripture! It is all in there.

---

9   As of the revision of this book, the chart has been revised yet again. This time, it is a plate with four different-sized "slices of pizza" (representing fruits, vegetables, grains, and protein) and a small circle (for dairy). Sorry to all you lovers of sweets! Check it out at https://naldc.nal.usda.gov/historical_dietary_guidance_digital.

It is inconceivable to the truly biblical counselor that Jesus Christ expects His church to develop a theology of counseling based on a hodgepodge of presuppositionally humanistic concepts (regardless of how much so-called truth they may contain). As far as the essentials of counseling are concerned, any "truth" not taught in the Word of God must either be wrong (and not truth at all) or unnecessary.

"Are you saying, then, that psychology has no value when it comes to counseling?"

No, I am not. I believe there is a place for Christians to utilize, in a very limited way, some of the research of secular *descriptive* psychology without resorting to integration. Let me begin with a brief review of the process of developing a systematic theology. This is important because biblical counseling is essentially practical theology.[10] It is not a theory of counseling but rather a theology of change (the theology of progressive sanctification—how man is transformed into the image of Christ).

Beginning with the biblical texts, systematic theologians apply scientific principles of interpretation (hermeneutics) to each relevant passage, determining and elucidating its meaning (exegesis). Then, all the relevant passages are systematized so that everything the Bible says about a particular topic is put together so that all the passages harmonize. Hence, everything the Holy Spirit has to say on the subject is understood in its historical context and applied by the believer (in the power of the Holy Spirit) to his life.

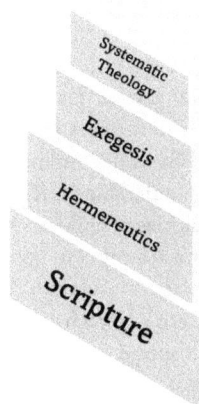

Systematic Theology

Exegesis

Hermeneutics

Scripture

---

10   One of my college instructors liked to use the term *peripatology* (from the Greek word *peripateo*, "to walk"), the study of the Christian walk, to describe practical theology.

Many helpful resources are utilized in the process of exegeting (and ultimately applying) the biblical text. Interpreters use the disciplines of archaeology, history, science, linguistics, logic, geography, and textual criticism to assist them in elucidating the meaning of the texts.

I believe we can use certain types of psychological data in much the same way theologians use these "uninspired" disciplines—as tools to help us better elucidate the meaning of a text[11] and perhaps even to motivate (provoke) us to search out more biblical truth.[12]

By using the secular data in this way, they (like archaeology, history, science, linguistics, geography, etc.) become the *servant* of the text and not equal to it. The veracity of these data is not viewed as infallible. Neither are they viewed as divinely authoritative— they are not viewed as "the Truth." They are employed in such a way that Scripture remains the master (and only present source of absolute truth). The data are subservient to it—not supplementing God's Word but rather elevating it to its rightful place as the only complete and authoritative textbook written specifically to provide answers to man's behavioral problems and the means for man's behavioral changes.

---

11   E.g., Paul says in 1 Cor. 13:11, "When I was a child, I used to speak like a child, think like a child, reason like a child." Some of the scientific data gleaned from developmental child psychology might be of some value in helping us understand a few of the distinctions between the speaking and reasoning abilities of children and adults. But again, we must remember that unsaved man's attempts to describe human behavior are inaccurate since he doesn't see man as God does (i.e., created sinner, redeemed sinner, regenerated person, etc.). So, what it amounts to is that all psychology can provide for us is uninspired hints, clues, and suggestions that we may explore and must correct.

12   I can't remember how many times I have read a piece of psychobabble that, because of some distorted but vaguely recognizable "bit of truth," motivated me to go back to the Bible to discover "the whole, unadulterated truth" and its various applications.

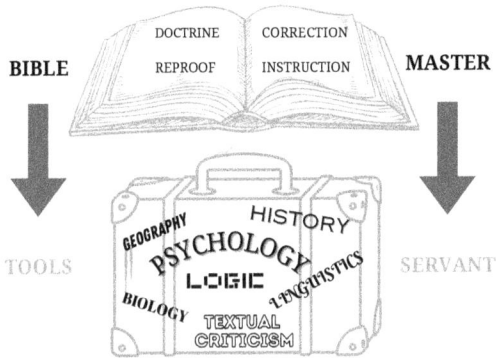

But can you imagine tearing a few pages out of a history, geography, or logic textbook and pasting them into your Bible to equate them to (ascribe to them the same level of authority as) each other?

"That is ludicrous! Those texts are not God-breathed. They aren't even in the same league."

Yet, that is essentially what integrationists do when, attempting to create a "unified whole," they supplement (augment, annex, enhance) Scripture with the so-called truth of psychology. Why do they do so? Again, it is because (at least in practice) they don't believe it has everything necessary to teach people how to change.

"But sometimes, you biblical counselors say things similar to 'behavior modification techniques' or 'cognitive therapy' or 'reality therapy.' It seems like you're borrowing from the competition."

May it never be! The fact is that we have had the Truth (the Word of God) for thousands of years. It is ours, not theirs! If, centuries after Jesus Christ gave the Truth to His church, some pagan psychiatrist, theorist, or "mental health professional" stumbled onto a bit of it, figured out how to utilize it with limited success, though he didn't fully understand it, and mixed it with error, having distorted it beyond almost all recognition, then please don't try to tell me that *we* borrowed it from *him*. *He* stole it from *us*. Yes, he was allowed by God to discover it, but then, because he left God out of his thinking, he twisted and misapplied it.

The Christian integrationist is right about one thing: to the extent that there is a measure (unverifiable) of truth mixed into his theory, the truth really is God's truth. The problem is that he doesn't quite understand the reality of the equation that while truth plus truth equals truth, truth plus error equals error. Neither, I am afraid, does he fully appreciate that "all error is the devil's error."

Let me say a word about the phrase *non-Christian content* in our presupposition. There is one especially perilous type of "content." What I am referring to is *unbiblical constructs*. Whether it is an anthropological construct (for example, organs of the soul such as the id, ego, superego, unconscious mind, or a deterministic personality trait that can only be discovered by some psychometric instrument), or a diagnostic category of "pathological" human behavior (such as some of the disorders categorized in the DSM-5), biblical counselors are suspicious of artificial constructs not built upon solid exegesis of Scripture. Instead, they reevaluate these constructs in light of Scripture to see if there might be a more biblical way to understand these ethereal entities. And when it is apparent that someone we are counseling interprets his problems through the lens of these man-made paradigms, we look for opportunities to disabuse him of the nomenclature that will point him in the wrong direction for the solutions to his problems.

Before I conclude this chapter, I would like you to think about one more thing. It has to do with the notion of general revelation (which, you remember, is where eclectic integrationists claim to get a good portion of their truth). If general revelation is not sufficient to save us (for that, we need *special* revelation), why do some suppose it is sufficient to sanctify us? According to the Bible, the truth revealed by God in general revelation is *limited* to a few things about God Himself and the fact that man (generally speaking) is in quite a bit of trouble with Him.[13] I have included in the appendix an emended chapter from a book by Jay Adams that sheds some light on the limits of general revelation and the distinction between what God has revealed through it and what man had discovered apart from it. What's the difference? If you don't know, don't stop here. Check out the appendix before you go on to the next presupposition.

---

13   The truth about God and man's hopeless condition given to us in general revelation is also given (but with much greater precision and comprehensiveness) in special revelation.

Presupposition 10

Expecting Results and Seeing Results

"What a loser!"

"I don't hold out much hope for her."

"He's been diagnosed with a mental disorder, so I don't expect him to ever really get better."

"Those two are so messed up, I doubt they will *ever* be able to make their marriage work."

Have you ever heard such sentiments expressed by pastors or Christian counselors?

"Yes, and I think it's awful. What kind of help could such a person offer people in distress?"

Then let me ask you, "Have you ever expressed such thoughts to yourself?"

"Ouch! Yes, I must confess that I have."

Thank you for being honest. I have also, on occasion, temporarily succumbed to similar faithless thoughts about those I was trying to help.

People who come for counseling need hope. They need to sense from you and me that we truly believe God is able to solve their seemingly hopeless problems.[1] As a counselor, the confidence (or lack of it) you possess in Christ and His Word is one of *your* communicable characteristics. Furthermore, for better or worse, it is often communicated unintentionally. Those you counsel soon pick up data from various verbal and nonverbal clues that you are either confident in biblical counseling or are uncertain whether it can help people as "messed up" as they are.

Presupposition number 10 simply states, **Counselors should expect and see results from biblical counseling.** "Faith is the assurance of things hoped for, the conviction of things not seen" (Heb. 11:1).

Let me ask you, Why should you, as a Christian counselor, have hope that your Christian counselee can change (no matter how "messed up" he is)? Why should you expect to see results? You should expect to see results because all conditions for your believing counselee to change have been met by God.

To begin with, you are dealing with a renewed person—someone who has been regenerated (quickened) by the Holy Spirit. The Spirit of God actually *lives* within him, making him capable not only of change but of changing in ways that please God. He can develop "proven character" (which brings about hope) because the love of God has been poured out within his heart through the Holy Spirit who was given to him (Rom. 5:4–6).

Then, there is the fact that he—not to mention you as his counselor—has been given the sufficient Word of God, which (as we have seen in a previous presupposition) contains everything he needs for life and godliness (2 Peter 1:3). "The law of the LORD is perfect [complete], restoring the soul" (Ps. 19:7). The Spirit working through the Word is the means God has ordained to bring about lasting change in the hearts and lives of God's elect.

---

1   One's ability to find hope in a "hopeless situation" is directly related to his ability to see God's hand in that situation. To the extent that your counselee can see (even if it is only by faith) what God is (or might be) up to in his life, he will have hope.

And if that were not enough, there is also the fact that your counselee has a counselor who is ministering the Word in the power of the Spirit. As a member of the body of Christ, you are a vital part of the hope your counselee has as he considers the resources God has given him to change. The Bible says that you, as a Spirit-filled believer, are "competent to counsel" other believers.

You might say, "Sometimes, I don't feel very competent to counsel myself, let alone someone else."

Neither do I. But that's when I remind myself of the promises of God and of the fact that I can't depend on (let alone follow) my feelings. And when I consider the competition (all those non-Christian counselors and counselors who are Christian but who do not follow a biblical counseling model in their attempts to help people change), I realize that even in my feebleness, I, by God's grace, have much more to offer than they do.

Let's zoom out a bit to consider one last item virtually all *obedient* Christian counselees (in the United States)[2] who want to change have going for them. It is really the big umbrella under which our last resource (a Spirit-filled biblical counselor) operates: the local church. As we will see in greater detail in a future presupposition, the local church is vital to the change process. It provides, among other things, Bible teaching, opportunities for corporate worship, loving Christian fellowship, the Lord's Table, accountability, a variety of role models, prayer support, and church discipline. All of these things contribute significantly to the believer's sanctification—the transformation, or change, into the image of Christ.

So, to what extent do you *now* believe that if your believing counselee obeys God, He will provide a biblical solution to

---

2 I'm adding this parenthesis and note while 38,000 feet above the Atlantic Ocean on my flight home from a visit to Europe where this statement doesn't often hold true. There are believers all over the world who do not currently have a biblical local church to attend. We who are privileged to live in the United States of America should count our blessings.

whatever problem he faces? Do you really believe such a counselee has at his disposal the unlimited power of God? I trust that what I have said so far has strengthened your faith. Let me give you a few more things to consider as you contemplate the kind of results you will see from your biblical counseling ministry in the following days and weeks.

You should expect to see change in your believing counselees because:

- "No temptation has overtaken him but such as is common to man; and God is faithful, who will not allow him to be tempted beyond what he is able, but with the temptation will provide the way of escape also, so that he will be able to endure it" (1 Cor. 10:13).

- Those you counsel (if they are truly born again) "can do all things through Him who strengthens [them]" (Phil. 4:13).

- God "is able to do far more abundantly beyond all that [your counselees] ask or think, according to the power that works within [them]" (Eph. 3:20).

- God's "divine power has granted to [them] everything pertaining to life and godliness, through the true knowledge of Him who called [them] by His own glory and excellence. For by these He has granted to [them] His precious and magnificent promises, so that by them [they] may become partakers of the divine nature, having escaped the corruption that is in the world by lust" (2 Peter 1:3–4).

Now, what are the practical implications of this presupposition? Let me give you three.

First, if you do not see results after a reasonable period, you should stop to evaluate what has hindered the results. Could it be that your counselee doesn't truly know the Lord? Is he not serious about change (e.g., Is he really willing to radically amputate those things in his life that have proven to be more of a temptation than he can handle)? Is it possible he has not told you everything you need to help him (like struggles with sin about which he is embarrassed to talk)? Could it be that he is not giving the Spirit his most powerful weapon (he is not internalizing enough of God's Word)? Are you certain the counsel you are giving him is biblically accurate? Have you missed the bull's-eye regarding the biblical diagnosis you are working with? In *Competent to Counsel*, Jay Adams has a very helpful appendix entitled "Fifty Failure Factors," which I commend to you should you not see the change you expect.[3]

Second, if the counselee does not follow God's directives, he should not be made to leave counseling before it is explained that he failed rather than God.

It is not that the Scriptures failed.

It is not that God failed.

It is not that the counselor failed,

but rather that the *counselee* failed to do what God requires.

Third, the results both you and your counselee should expect to see are different from the kind of results other counselors see. One of the things that sets biblical counseling apart from other forms of counseling is the total transformation of the one being counseled. Unlike the Skinnerian school of thought, biblical counseling is not content to facilitate a change only in an individual's *behavior*. Nor are we satisfied (like many in the Cognitive Therapy camp) with simply seeing people change their thought processes. And while we (contrary to what you might have heard) do value a person's feelings as a significant part of the human experience, we, unlike some Rational Emotive theoreticians, do not primarily target these for change.[4] But more than this, we are also concerned

---

3   Jay E. Adams, *Competent to Counsel* (Grand Rapids: Zondervan, 2009).
4   We target those things in the life of our counselees that we believe generate feelings (i.e., his thoughts, words, and actions).

with helping the counselee correct any hurtful (unbiblical) values, desires, and motives that displease God and contribute greatly to his misery. Indeed, only the Word of God can diagnose and correct problems at this level "for the word of God is living and active and sharper than any two-edged sword, and piercing as far as the division of soul and spirit, of both joints and marrow, and able to judge the thoughts and *intentions of the heart*" (Heb. 4:12).

Our job is to train those we counsel how to be conformed to (totally transformed into) the image of Christ. This means we don't just teach them how to *talk* and *behave* like Christ but also how to *think* and *be motivated* as He is. We have (in the Bible) "the mind of Christ" (1 Cor. 2:16).

So, the next time you catch yourself telling yourself that you don't think your believing counselee can change, you will need to change your own mind about what he has going for him before you attempt to lead him into repentance.

Presupposition 11

── Discipline and the Local Church ──

How many times do you suppose the concept of church discipline is mentioned in the New Testament?

"Well, let's see. There's the classic passage, Matthew 18:15–17. And then there is the fellow in 1 Corinthians 5 who was sexually involved with his stepmother. Oh yeah, and the passage in 2 Corinthians 2 where presumably that same guy is restored to the church. And, I don't know—I suppose we could count the Ananias and Sapphira account as a form of radical church discipline. I'm probably missing a few. Okay, I give up! Exactly how many are there?"

I will try to refresh your memory a bit. But before I do, allow me to introduce our eleventh presupposition: **Biblical counseling requires and includes church discipline when it is biblically necessary. Thus, biblical counseling should ultimately be done under the local church.**

The concept of church disciple is quite unpopular today—especially in some evangelical circles. I lost count long ago of the pastors I've met who were very interested in biblical counseling until they began to ponder the implications of this presupposition. And I have heard dozens of reasons (excuses, really) pastors give why it "would not work" in their churches.

Nevertheless, church discipline is inextricably woven into the fabric of biblical counseling. Let's consider the most basic passage on this matter in the Bible. As you read, notice the words I have italicized to bring out the counseling elements of this passage:

> And if your brother sins, *go and reprove him in private*; if he listens to you, you have won your brother. But if he does not listen to you, *take one or two more with you*, so that *by the mouth of two or three witnesses every fact may be confirmed.* And if he refuses to listen to them, *tell it to the church*; and if he refuses to listen even to the church, let him be to you as a Gentile and a tax gatherer. (Matt. 18:15–17)

Jay Adams points out in his classic work, the *Handbook for Church Discipline*, that there is an assumed first step (self-control on the part of the sinning "brother") which, if followed, would, in most cases, make all the others unnecessary.

Corrective Discipline

There are five steps to corrective discipline. They may be best understood by careful study of this diagram:

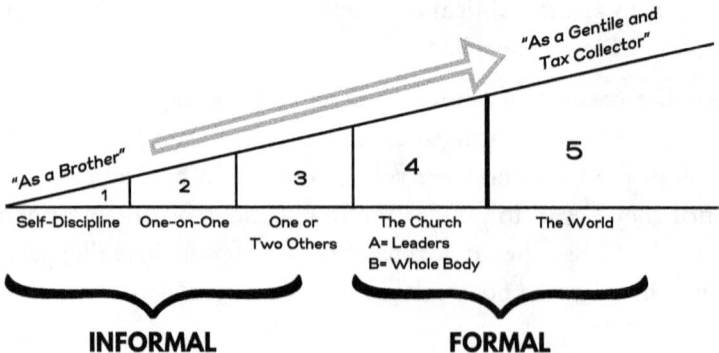

The middle three steps of the five-step process involve counseling.

Step two: "individual counseling:" *go and reprove him in private.*

Step three: "group counseling":[5] *take one or two more with you, so that by the mouth of two or three witnesses every fact may be confirmed.*

Step four: "family counseling": *tell it to the church.*[6]

Jesus knew some counseling problems could not be solved apart from church discipline. Did you get that? The reason[7] there are so many passages in the Bible relating to church discipline is because some people will not change apart from church discipline.[8] It's just that simple! This is yet one more reason why people who don't counsel biblically are not playing (counseling) with a full deck.

Now, of course, this doesn't mean that everyone who is the beneficiary of church discipline will change.[9] But many of them

---

5   Although we in the biblical counseling movement are concerned about the abuses of "group counseling" (which typically arise if all parties are not present so that the "group counseling session" becomes a "group gossip or slander session"), when Matt. 18:15–17 is followed, a scenario arises in which, unlike most group counseling sessions where these is one counselor and a number of counselees, there is a need for several counselors and only one counselee.

6   The purpose of this step is so that the entire church family may admonish (that is, counsel) the wayward brother (2 Thess. 3:14–15; 1 Thess. 5:14).

7   Of course, this is not the only or even the most important purpose of discipline. The *glory of God* and the *purity of the church* are two of several other reasons why God has instituted this process.

8   I have often wondered how many counseling problems were actually eliminated when churches regularly exercised discipline. Between eliminating problems that do not fester because the entire church understands and actively pursues and rescues members who have been overtaken by sin, to protecting the rest of the body from dangerous people joining the church because they know what they will be in for should their sin be exposed, I dare say that perhaps as many as 40 percent of serious church problems would never materialize.

9   I say *beneficiary* with all sincerity. Church discipline is a blessing. I would personally never want to place myself and my family in a church that would rob us of such protection and blessing.

will (as the fellow in 2 Corinthians 2 did, of whom the apostle Paul said, "Sufficient for such a one is this punishment which was inflicted by the majority, so that on the contrary you should rather forgive and comfort him").

"Okay, but what about those passages you mentioned? How many of them are there?"

There are quite a few. To begin with, all the verses that deal with one-on-one confrontation (such as Luke 17:3; Gal. 6:1; James 5:19) can rightly be placed under step one of Matthew 18:15. But a good number of other New Testament passages address the other phases of the process.

In Romans 16:17, Paul admonishes the entire church family to keep their eye "on those who cause dissensions and hindrances contrary to the teaching which you learned, and turn away from them."

In 1 Corinthians 4:19 and 21, he tells them of his intention to deal with some who were troubling the body. "But I will come to you soon, if the Lord wills, and I shall find out, not the words of those who are arrogant but their power. . . . What do you desire? Shall I come to you with a rod, or with love and a spirit of gentleness?"

Later on, he gives them a similar warning in 2 Corinthians 10:11 and 13:1–2:

> Let such a person consider this, that what we are in word by letters when absent, such persons we are also in deed when present. . . . This is the third time I am coming to you. Every fact is to be confirmed by the testimony of two or three witnesses. I have previously said when present the second time, and though now absent I say in advance to those who have sinned in the past and to all the rest as well, that if I come again I will not spare anyone.

First Thessalonians 5:14 seems to be another one of those "family counseling" scenarios—perhaps falling into that slot after the church has been told but just before the final (excommunication) phase of discipline. "We urge you, brethren, admonish the unruly." The same slot probably fits 2 Thessalonians 3:6, 14–15 as well. "Now we command you, brethren, in the name of our Lord Jesus Christ, that you keep away from every brother who leads an unruly life and not according to the tradition which you received from us. . . . If anyone does not obey our instruction in this letter, take special note of that person and do not associate with him, so that he will be put to shame. Yet do not regard him as an enemy, but admonish him as a brother."

And then there are Hymenaeus and Alexander, whom Paul "handed over to Satan, so that they will be taught not to blaspheme" (1 Tim. 1:19–20).

And let's not forget the specific instructions given on how to (quickly) deal with divisive people in Titus 3:10–11: "Reject a factious man after a first and second warning, knowing that such a man is perverted and is sinning, being self-condemned."

Finally (not that my list is an exhaustive one—I said I would try to "refresh your memory *a bit*"), there is John's promise to deal with Diotrephes in 3 John 10: "For this reason, if I come, I will call attention to his deeds which he does, unjustly accusing us with wicked words; and not satisfied with this, he himself does not receive the brethren, either, and he forbids those who desire to do so and puts them out of the church."

Here is a little chart Jay Adams put together that places the relevant passages under the final stages or phases of the Matthew 18:15–17 process.

—— Stage 4-B ——

"As a Brother"

II Thess. 3:15

IN THE CHURCH

☑ Don't Mix - - - II Thess. 3:14; I Cor 5:9,11
☑ Don't Eat - - - I Cor. 5:11
☑ Mark Him - - - II Thess. 3:14
☑ Counsel Him - -- Gal. 6:1; II Thess. 3:15

—— Stage 5 ——

"As a Heathen and Tax Collector"

Mt. 18:17

OUTSIDE THE
CHURCH

☑ Remove Him - - - I Cor. 5:2
☑ Clean Out the Leaven - - I Cor. 5:7
☑ Get Him Out of the Midst - - - I Cor 5:13
☑ Let Him Be as a Heathen & Tax Collector - - - Mt. 18:17
☑ I Have Handed Them Over to Satan - - - I Tim. 1:20
☑ Deliver This Person to Satan - - - I Cor. 5:5

Copyright © Dr. Jay E. Adams 1996

The second part of our presupposition concerns the connection between biblical counseling and the local church. In a previous chapter, I mentioned that the local church is one of the three most powerful resources God has given us for change—the Holy Spirit and the Scriptures being the other two.

In over thirty-five years of biblical counseling, I have had the opportunity to work in both local church and parachurch counseling centers. I prefer to minister in the former rather than the latter for reasons which may be obvious to some of you but which I don't have time to get into right now. The only points I do want to make in this chapter are that (1) every church is (or should be) a "counseling center,"[10] and (2) parachurch centers are only valid to the extent that they truly support the church—not primarily by counseling its people (for this is really the calling of pastors and elders in the local church) but by *training* its leaders to counsel biblically and by *producing material* that local churches may use in their counseling. In other words, all churches are counseling centers, but parachurch counseling ministries, to be biblical, should function more as "counselor-training centers" than as merely "counseling centers."[11]

Biblical counseling is something that God calls pastors and shepherds to do as a part of their life's calling. "The man of God" mentioned in 2 Timothy 3:17 who is "equipped for every good work" by the Scriptures is the shepherd: "All Scripture is inspired by God and profitable for teaching, for reproof, for correction, for training in righteousness; so that the man of God may be adequate, equipped for every good work" (vv. 16–17).

---

10   I am currently the (full-time) pastor of counseling at Christ Covenant in Atlanta. We have a "counseling center" that offers free counseling to our members. The church is exploding with growth. As I write this, I am not able to immediately see everyone in our congregation who want and need to see me. They must be placed on a waiting list. We are training and certifying other counselors as quickly and responsibly as we know how. Our hope is that, as we do so, we will be able to open up the Center for Biblical Counseling (as we call it) to minister to those outside our congregation. But whether any given church has a formal counseling center, because counseling is the function of the local church and the calling of each pastor/elder (as we will see in presupposition 12), each church should function, albeit if only informally, as a "counseling center." The local church is the context in which (the umbrella under which) spiritual counseling is to be given, according to Scripture.

11   I am also serving as the director of Competent to Counsel International (competenttocounsel.org), which is an international training center with the Association of Certified Biblical Counselors. While we do offer counseling, we do so with the understanding that trainees (pastors and students who want to learn how to counsel from Scripture) may be in each session. We also offer local and international training classes and workshops on counseling related topics. Additionally, we have produced and posted additional resources to help counselors and those they counsel.

The context in which God calls these men is the local church with *all* its sanctifying resources. While parachurch organizations are helpful (and sometimes necessary), they are not God-ordained institutions and should not be expected to function as local churches. They can't play with the whole deck of cards, they don't have the whole loaf of bread, and they can't swallow the whole enchilada. Only the local church has what the counselee needs to maximize his counseling experience.

But what of parachurch counseling centers? Are they an unbiblical construct? Not when functioning primarily as "counselor-training centers." I have spent more years "directing" parachurch counseling ministries than local church ministries. One of my constant struggles (much more so in the parachurch model) is trying to minister to churches without having them turn my centers into repositories (dumping grounds) for their hurting people. It's not that I didn't want to help them as much as I possibly could. I just didn't want them to "farm out" all their counseling cases to me because they were unequipped or unwilling to do the sometimes agonizing ministry of counseling—a ministry to which God had called *them*. I can't recall how often I have told church leaders who attended our counseling courses, "I hope you (local area churches) force me to close up shop and move to another city where I can start all over because you all have your own church counseling centers." Wouldn't that be wonderful? Although that has not yet happened—and because of the feeble condition of today's churches, it probably never will—God has given me the privilege to witness something of a "nouthetic revival" in the town where I now minister. How exciting is that?

What Does This Mean?

What are the practical implications of this presupposition? First, those you counsel should be encouraged to attend church regularly. It is not good to be disconnected. As I explained in the last chapter, "the local church is vital to the change process.

It provides, among other things, Bible teaching, opportunities for corporate worship, loving Christian fellowship, the Lord's Table, accountability, a variety of role models, prayer support, and church discipline. All of these things contribute significantly to the believer's sanctification—the transformation, or change, into the image of Christ."[12]

After elucidating some of the benefits of regular church attendance and membership, I might ask some of my unchurched counselees, "Would you be willing to make a commitment to me (if not, to the Lord)? For at least as long as you are counseling with me, I would like you to attend at least once weekly a Bible-believing church. If you don't know of a good one, I would love for you to start attending here. I would also love to introduce you to some friends of mine. Do you think you are ready to make such a commitment?"[13]

Second, as a rule, counselees should be encouraged to inform their church leaders that they are seeking outside help. (In fact, they should be encouraged to seek them out first, should the need for counseling arise in the future.) I make it my goal to try to work as closely as I can with the pastors who send their flock to our counseling center. They are always welcome to sit in and participate in my sessions.

Third, most churches would benefit from having others in the body assist the pastor with his counseling load. Counseling may properly be done not just by but also under the supervision of the elders. Indeed, Paul expressed his confidence that the Romans were "competent to counsel one another" (Rom. 15:14).

I mentioned earlier that I have heard many excuses from pastors for not practicing church discipline. You might appreciate

---

12   *The Journal of Modern Ministry*, Volume 4, Issue 1, 95.

13   If the counselee is not ready for such a commitment, depending on his reason, I will usually remind him that in the paperwork he signed as a prerequisite for counseling, he agreed this would be a requirement for our counseling him.

looking at some of the most common excuses and the biblical counterarguments I have found effective.

Rationalizations for Not Practicing Church Discipline	Biblical Counterargument *for* Practicing Church Discipline
"It will not work."	Pragmatism is not the basis for our action. The Word of God is. And Matthew 18:15–17 is not optional—it's a command.
	Furthermore, it *will* work. It may not bring the contumacious brother to repentance, but if done properly, it will bring glory to God. Christians witness to the lost, knowing that not all those they give the gospel to will be saved. Yet because they are commanded to proclaim the good news, they do so—knowing that God will someday receive glory from their obedience even though not everyone to whom they witnessed believed the gospel.
"It would be 'judging.'"	Of course, it would! It is your job to do so. "For I . . . have already judged him who has so committed this, as though I were present" (1 Cor. 5:3).

"My elder board is not behind me."	"This is a valid argument up to a point. For two (or four or sixteen) to work together, they must agree. But more often than not, this line is an excuse. Sure, it may take time to persuade the rest of the men to see the importance and non-optional nature of the church discipline process. Perhaps even more time will be required to teach the church all the Bible says about the matter. But to simply give up on your church leadership and turn a blind eye to those in the church who need to be rescued and to allow the church to be contaminated and the reputation of Christ to be harmed is inexcusable.[14] More importantly, it is sin. "Therefore, to one who knows the right thing to do and does not do it, to him it is sin" (James 4:17).
Other people in the church have similar problems	This is a difficult situation, one that probably requires a book of its own. The bottom line is that it may be necessary to deal with several individuals at once if there are those in the church who, for years, have been allowed to skate by without discipline. The best solution may be for the church leaders to make an appointment with these individuals, asking their forgiveness for not following through with the necessary discipline earlier. Then, interview them to determine the extent to which they may have repented of their previous sins, and if they have not, to resume (or reinitiate) the Matthew 18:15–17 process.

---

14   It is what a hireling does, not a true shepherd!

"Our church is not ready to practice church discipline."	Your church is not ready to obey the Bible? It's your job to get them ready!
"It could cause divisions."	The truth is divisive! Obedience to Christ and His Word is more important than an artificial unity built on disobedience and compromise. A lack of discipline will ultimately contribute to greater disunity.[15]
"It will cause people to ask, 'How can I trust the spiritual leaders in confidence with any sin problem I might have?'"	The very fact that an individual is willing to go to a spiritual leader to get help to conquer a sin is evidence that he has already begun demonstrating "fruit unto repentance." Discipline is reserved for people who have no intention or desire to be delivered from sin. Also, confidentiality and friendship are not more important than godliness and God's glory. For this reason, Christians who counsel cannot give absolute confidentiality to those they counsel. To do so would be to necessarily promise to disobey Matthew 18:15–18.
"Our church is not in the discipline business; we are in the business of forgiveness."[16]	Then you are in the wrong business. And you are being shortsighted. One of the purposes of church discipline is forgiveness.

15   "Church Discipline," study notes from a workshop held at the 1986 Shepherd's Conference at Grace Community Church, Sun Valley, California.

16   The story behind this one makes my blood boil to this day. A man was excommunicated by one local church for leaving his wife for totally unbiblical reasons. The man went across town and attempted to join another church. When the pastor of the disciplining church called the pastor of the second church to inform him of the situation (to warn him, in other words, that he was about to welcome a Jonah into his boat) and to ask him to send the man back to reconcile with his church and wife, the pastor allegedly used this line.

"We might be sued!"	"There is no fear in love, but perfect love casts out fear" (1 John 4:18).
	We cannot allow the fear of potential consequences to keep us from loving God (by obeying His commands) or from loving our neighbor (by not helping to extricate him from the ditch into which he has fallen).
	In this litigious world, lawsuits seem to be filed for almost anything. But it would be challenging for a plaintive to win such a suit against a church that truly follows biblical procedures.
	Additional precautions can be taken to help minimize the risk of these kinds of lawsuits. Ken Sande, for example, has published several good resources to help churches practice biblical discipline without exposing themselves to unnecessary risks.

I will leave you with a little slogan I learned years ago that summarizes what I have tried to say in this chapter: "Counseling: keep it of the Bible, keep it in the church."

Presupposition 12

—————— CALLING AND EQUIPPING ——————

A S WE COME TO THE final presupposition, let me ask you a question. Who does God require, equip, and call to do the work of biblical counseling? Presupposition 12 gives us the answer: **God requires and equips all believers to counsel. Additionally, God holds the officers of His church responsible to counsel as a part of their life calling.**

All Christians do some counseling. As we saw a few pages back, the process of discipline (in which all believers are obligated to participate) begins with a one-on-one "counseling session": "If your brother sins, go and show him his fault in private; if he listens to you, you have won your brother" (Matt. 18:15).

Beyond this, the Bible addresses the non-optional nature of (informal) counseling in other places. Please keep in mind as you read the rest of this chapter that there are several other verbs in the New Testament for counseling besides *noutheteo*:[1]

—————

1   E.g., *parainéō; protrépō; parakaléō; paideúō; hupodeíknumi; chrēmatízō; sumbouleúō; sunistáō / sunístēmi; epitimáō.* Dr. Adams chose to associate the biblical counseling movement with this term because, of all the words available, *noutheteo* was the best and most complete term to describe biblical counseling.

Brethren, even if anyone is caught in any trespass, you who are spiritual, restore such a one in a spirit of gentleness; *each one* looking to yourself, so that you too will not be tempted. (Gal. 6:1)

Be on your guard! If your brother sins, rebuke him; and if he repents, forgive him. (Luke 17:3)

Let the word of Christ richly dwell within you, with all wisdom teaching and admonishing one another with psalms *and* hymns *and* spiritual songs, singing with thankfulness in your hearts to God. (Col. 3:16)

We urge you, brethren, admonish the unruly, encourage the fainthearted, help the weak, be patient with everyone. (1 Thess. 5:14)

Then, there are those general, nonobligatory New Testament passages that teach that all believers are at least potentially competent to do counseling:

And concerning you, my brethren, I myself also am convinced that you yourselves are full of goodness, filled with all knowledge and able also to admonish one another. (Rom. 15:14)

Blessed be the God and Father of our Lord Jesus Christ, the Father of mercies and God of all comfort [or assistance], who comforts us in all our affliction so that we will be able to comfort [assist] those who are in any affliction with the comfort [assistance] with which we ourselves are comforted [assisted] by God. (2 Cor. 1:3–4)

So, counseling for the Christian is prospectively a part of his calling—someday, in some way, God will call on him or her to counsel another. Moreover, at some level, everyone who is indwelt by the Spirit of God is already competent to counsel other believers. Of course, there are a couple of conditions that all counseling

Christians should strive to meet. In Romans 15:14:

> Paul set forth goodness and knowledge as qualifications
> for good counselors. These qualities are essential; nothing
> less makes one "competent to counsel" (Williams). Paul
> recognized that any Christian may engage in nouthetic
> counseling so long as he possesses the qualities of good-
> ness and knowledge. . . .
>
> Nouthetic ability involves goodness and knowledge in large
> measure (fullness). Preeminently, a nouthetic counselor
> must be conversant with the Scriptures. This is one rea-
> son why properly equipped ministers may make excellent
> counselors. A good seminary education, rather than med-
> ical school or a degree in clinical psychology, is the most
> fitting background for a counselor. Real counseling involves
> the imparting of information. . . . Goodness embraces both
> the involvement and empathetic concern. . . . It also com-
> prises an enthusiasm of life in which Christ is apparent,
> and which thereby communicates hope to the counselee.[2]

The second point of our twelfth presupposition expresses
the truth that God uniquely calls church leaders to do the work
of biblical counseling as a part of their pastoral responsibilities.
Hebrews 13:17 is not only instructive to the church member
but also to the church officer: "Obey your leaders and submit to
them, for they *keep watch over your souls* as those who will give
an account. Let them do this with joy and not with grief, for this
would be unprofitable for you."

What does it mean to "keep watch" over the souls of the
saints? The Greek construction of this word (ἀγρυπνέω), which
means to be watchful (attentive), is present and active, indicating
continuous action on the part of the shepherd. This connotes

---

2   Jay E. Adams, *Competent to Counsel* (Grand Rapids: Zondervan, 2009),
    60–61. Dr. Adams also adds a third condition for a biblical counselor, found
    in Col. 3:16: wisdom (p. 62).

an almost hypervigilant mindset on the part of the shepherd. In other words, it's not a matter of waiting around until some problem in the flock materializes but of proactively looking for signs of a problem before it develops. A good shepherd will regularly examine his sheep. He will keep his eyes peeled for indications of sickness. He will notice any unusual smells or sounds emanating from the sheep's bodies. He will check their fleeces, running his hands under the wool to check for unusual lumps, scabs, or insects. He will notice things that don't look normal—not to find problems where none exist but to deal with any real issues before they become serious. The point is that shepherding involves a level of intimacy with the sheep that too few church leaders are willing to achieve. Shepherding can be dirty work. All this necessitates counseling.

Paul's example of an elder who is intimately involved with his flock can be seen in Acts 20:18–21:

> And when they had come to him, he said to them,
> "You yourselves know, from the first day that I set foot in Asia, how I was with you the whole time, serving the Lord with all humility and with tears and with trials which came upon me through the plots of the Jews; how I did not shrink from declaring to you anything that was profitable, and teaching you publicly and from house to house, solemnly testifying to both Jews and Greeks of repentance toward God and faith in our Lord Jesus Christ."

Paul was not the kind of shepherd who locked himself in the study for thirty-five hours per week, only to come out to preach publicly on the Lord's Day (and perhaps on Wednesday evening). Instead, he would minister publicly *and from house to house*. That is, he would minister the Word to entire congregations as well as to smaller groups and individuals. (Although generally speaking, I can appreciate the sentiment behind the phrase "the primacy of preaching," I can't help but think that Paul would have preferred the phrase "the primacy of the ministry of the Word.")

Like a skilled marksman, the man of God knows how to wield his Bible as a shotgun (when, from the pulpit, he sprays a broad pattern of birdshot, hoping to hit as many consciences as possible) or to utilize it as a 7mm-08 rifle (when, in the counseling office, he carefully places the crosshairs of his Austrian-made Kahles scope on the exact spot where it will have the greatest impact).

Few people have bolded this point as John Calvin in his commentary on the book of Acts:

> *Publicly, and throughout every house.* This is the second point, that he [the apostle Paul] did not only teach all men in the congregation, but also every one privately, as every man's necessity did require. For Christ hath not appointed pastors upon this condition, that they only teach the church in general in the open pulpit; but that they may take charge of every particular sheep, that they may bring back to the sheepfold those who wander and go astray, that they may strengthen those who are discouraged and weak, that they may cure the sick, that they may lift up and set on foot the feeble (Ezek. 34:4) for common doctrine will oftentimes wax cold, unless it be holpen [helped] with private admonition.
>
> Wherefore, the negligence of those men is inexcusable, who, having made one sermon, as if they had done their task, live all the rest of their time idly; as if their voice were shut up within the church walls, seeing that so soon as they departed thence, they be dumb.[3]

Perhaps pastors who don't counsel because they believe they are called only to preach should be challenged to preach a few

---

3   *The Library of Christian Classics, Vol. XXI, Calvin: Institutes of the Christian Religion,* ed. John T. McNeill, trans. Ford Lewis Battles (Louisville, KY: Westminister John Knox Press, 1960), IV.i.4, 2:1016.

sermons from the books of Jeremiah and Ezekiel about shepherding—noting especially what God thinks of (and promises to do to) shepherds who don't minister to individual needs of the sheep.

What was it that characterized the false shepherds of Israel? They were primarily concerned with their own needs,[4] not those of the flock. They were so concerned about their own advancement and enrichment that they neglected the sheep. They wouldn't invest the time and effort necessary to care for the weak, sickly, and diseased or seek after those scattered and lost. Their lack of attention to the individual needs of the sheep resulted in some of the flock becoming "food for every beast of the field" (Ezek. 34:3–5).

Our churches are filled with spiritually weak, sick, and diseased sheep. Many of these flocks have shepherds who possess in the Word of God the cure for all such spiritual maladies but who, because they are only interested in feeding the sheep, will not care for their wounds.

Other passages in the New Testament speak of counseling being a part of the work of the ministry. Notice, for example, the counseling connotations implied in these two verses from the Pastoral Epistles:

> For the overseer must be above reproach as God's steward, not self-willed, not quick-tempered, not addicted to wine, not pugnacious, not fond of sordid gain, but hospitable, loving what is good, sensible, just, devout, self-controlled, holding fast the faithful word which is in accordance with the teaching, so that he will be able both to exhort in sound doctrine and to refute those who contradict. (Titus 1:7–9)

> The Lord's bond-servant must not be quarrelsome, but be kind to all, able to teach, patient when wronged, with gen-

---

4   I can't help wonder how many "I don't counsel because I've got to spend almost all of my time working on my sermon" pastors are really more concerned about their *reputation* as a pulpiteer than they are about caring for the individual needs of the flock.

tleness correcting those who are in opposition,* if perhaps God may grant them repentance leading to the knowledge of the truth, and they may come to their senses *and escape* from the snare of the devil, having been held captive by him to do his will. (2 Tim. 2:24–26)

So, while all Christians are "competent to counsel," all shepherds are "called to counsel." And if you are called, you should be equipped. But are you? If you are not, training centers all across the United States (some of which even offer video training) can furnish you with the right equipment. For more information, go to biblicalcounseling.com or iabc.net and click on "Training Centers."

Never forget that you have all you need in the Word of God (and through the Holy Spirit) to not only *feed* God's flock but also to *cure* its spiritually sick. I pray that as a result of what you have just read, the Holy Spirit will enable you to use the Bible more effectively and confidently in your shepherding ministry.

Appendix

THE INSUFFICIENCY OF
—————— GENERAL REVELATION ——————
FOR SANCTIFICATION[1]

Jay E. Adams

INTEGRATIONISTS ARE CLEAR about one thing: they believe that psychological "truths" have been revealed by God. How can they say so? By appealing to the category of "general revelation." For instance, here is what one of them said when writing about me: "He apparently never even thought of the notion that all truth is God's truth, has equal warrant, whether truth from nature or scripture."[2] The error in this statement about me made by J. Harold Ellens is of no consequence. It just shows how little some of those who write know about nouthetic counseling. What is important is his comment that truth from nature and Scripture have "equal warrant." It is this sort of thinking with which we

---

1 This article has been adapted and condensed from chapter 5 of *Is All Truth God's Truth?* by Jay E. Adams (Stanley, NC: Timeless Texts, 2003). Used by permission.

2 Douglas Bookman, *The Scriptures and Biblical Counseling*, John MacArthur and Wayne Mack, *Introduction to Biblical Counseling* (Dallas: Word, 1994), 71. Bookman retorts, "Such a charge is simply ludicrous. Adams has written at copious lengths about this specific issue." He is, of course, correct, and Ellens is wrong.

shall be concerned in the present chapter. Ellens is not alone. Both he and William F. English think that God reveals truth through "nature" or general revelation. But, listen to English: "Truth derived from the study of any segment of general revelation, whether psychology, or any other field, is not as trustworthy as the truth found in the Scriptures."[3] Two problems arise as we consider these statements.

They differ from the Christian view at a crucial point: Is truth really Truth? Ellens thinks so, referring to the slogan we have been considering and calling the supposed "truth" derived from general revelation "Truth." For him, therefore, psychological truth is "God's truth." One can only wonder at the thinking of English at this point when he, too, speaks of "truth derived from . . . general revelation," which is "not as trustworthy as the truth found in the Scriptures." He proposes, therefore, the "filtering" of "psychological truth through biblical truth."

Is "truth" Truth?

What is truth for English? How can anyone think that "truth" may be untrustworthy—especially if he adheres to the slogan, "All truth is God's truth"? Truth is Truth. If it is God's Truth given by general revelation, then it cannot be considered as less "trustworthy" than His Truth given in special revelation (the Bible). How can any truth be more or less "trustworthy" and still be God's Truth? All of God's Truth is trustworthy. And, if the Truth derived from general revelation is from God, how can one speak of filtering it? You can't filter out error from God's Truth because in His Truth there is none! Truth is Truth—but English doesn't seem to think so. He has two kinds of "truth."[4] How can

---

3   Bookman, 91.

4   Compare H. Newton Malony's analysis of Gary Collins' view: "He distinguishes 'TRUTH' from 'truth,' and recognizes that because the various data under examination are from different sources (some revealed and some empirically derived), tension is bound to exist between Christian and

there be such? What does he mean by *less* trustworthy truth? If it is less trustworthy, but still God's truth, then God's Word (at least in part) is untrustworthy. How can this be? The sloppy thinking that is often found in the integrationist movement makes it difficult to critique. Truth, if it "truly" is Truth, is always trustworthy—simply because it is Truth.

What "truth"?

There are many non-Christians who talk of truth as if every man has his own truth. While I am sure that English does not believe this, it is necessary to warn those who read him of the danger of this sort of speaking because it can easily lead to thinking the way these unbelievers do. When he says that truth must be "filtered," he cannot possibly mean that such truth is Truth; otherwise it could not be called truth—could it? You don't filter truth in order to obtain the truth that is within truth. The language used is patently ridiculous.

What he seems to be trying to say (however badly) is that non-truth has been mixed with Truth (that supposedly comes from God in general revelation) and must be filtered out of the mix. But his words seem to say that truths mixed with lesser truths have to be separated. The difficulty that he has is simply this: he has called general revelation a source of "psychological truth," but he can't bring himself to believe that general revelation is really *Revelation*. And *that* is the crux of the matter.

Is General Revelation Really "Revelation"?

Is the so-called psychological "truth" that one finds in nature revelation? Appealing to "general revelation," as most integrationists do in order to enhance the credibility of their theories, raises serious questions. As English's words indicate, this is a slippery thing to get hold of. It is almost like those who

non-Christian psychologists." Collins and Malony, *Psychology and Theology, Prospects for Integration* (Nashville: Abingdon, 1981), 90.

speak of mental illness, sometimes stressing the word "illness" in order to snatch counselees away from biblical counselors and, at other times, stressing the word "mental" whenever they wish to say what should be done in counseling instead of sending them to a physician. I once spoke at the Rosemead Graduate School and in the question-and-answer session that followed, an attendee said, "You can't deal with persons who are mentally ill." My reply to this psychologist (who evidently thought the "mentally ill" were in his domain) was "Neither can you if they are truly ill! Psychologists are not doctors either." Sometimes such people find it convenient to stress one thing, sometimes another.

Now, something of that sort happens when integrationists speak of revelation and of something less trustworthy. English has called the something-less-than-trustworthy material revelation; others, more astute, when convenient, find it necessary to do something else. But when these same people want to gain credibility for their views, they speak of this material as revelation from God which has "equal warrant" for acceptation as does biblical Truth.

The confusion over these matters is obvious. But that confusion is endemic to integrationism. That is because they try but, as they say, "You can't have it both ways." Either general revelation is truly revelation, or it isn't. If revelation, clearly there is nothing to filter. It is all as pure as the words of Scripture (special revelation).

Where Is the "truth"?

All revelation from God is inerrant. This fact poses a new problem for the integrationist. He can call some theory, idea, or method supposedly discovered in nature "God's Truth" if he wishes, but if he thinks for a minute, how is he to establish it as such? In no other field of endeavor has there been so much disagreement. Psychologists retool throughout their lifetimes to keep up with the latest newly uncovered system (or parts thereof). Think of all those systems that were once called God's Truth that have been discarded![5] Gary Almy, MD, remarks, "Lacking solid foundation, one movement after another has come and gone over the course of psychotherapy's one-hundred-year history."[6] Others, tired of the retooling process, cling to one or another outmoded or debunked system. How could this be true if any were "psychological truth" that has been revealed? Which theory is True, and which is not? Why should there be a mixture of truth and error if God has truly revealed *truth*? Did God want to confuse us? Revelation, whether General or Special, is always inerrant. In special revelation, we can turn with confidence to any part of it and be sure that we are dealing with Truth. In dealing with nature, on the other hand, integrationists tell us that we must separate truth from error, revealed materials from nonrevealed materials. If there were Truth mixed with error, who gets to decide what is revelation and what is not?

---

5   The situation is almost as bad as faddish nutritional and health advice. Views change with the next article you read. What should one believe? In the *Spartanburg Herald Journal,* this humorous article that sets up the problem appeared: "The Japanese eat very little fat and suffer fewer heart attacks than the British and Americans. The French eat a lot of fat and also suffer fewer heart attacks than the British or Americans. The Japanese drink very little red wine and suffer fewer heart attacks than the British or Americans. The Italians drink excessive amounts of red wine and suffer fewer heart attacks than the British or Americans. In conclusion, eat and drink what you like. Speaking English apparently is what kills you."

   William L. Isley, MD, writes, "The medical literature contains thousands of articles which have now been corrected, disregarded, or even have been shown to be flagrantly wrong despite the presence of a 'statistically signicant *p* value for the results.'" *The Journal of Biblical Ethics in Medicine,* Vol 5, No 4, 65–66.

6   Gary Almy, *How Christian Is Christian Counseling?* (Wheaton, IL: Crossway, 2000), 241. Almy continues: "It is characteristic of the history of psychotherapy that new ideas constantly push old ones from the scene. . . . Before the Recovery Memory Therapy movement of the mid-1980s, one version of psychotherapy after another had come and gone in faddish ways" (244, 248).

Psychology Not a Science

There is trouble in River City! Psychology, thought of as a science, must agree to science's fundamental premise that nothing is final, all is in flux. What today is considered a fact, tomorrow is rejected as disproved. This is true of many once-cherished views. Once, people believed in the Phlogiston theory of negative weight. Bringing this concept into some mathematical equations helped them explain facts having to do with the weight of burned substances before and after the burning process. Since then, it has been held that in burning, something also enters into the material burned, thus causing the residue to be heavier than before burning. Who knows whether or not there will be a later modification of this view? Science changes precisely because, unlike revelation, there is no assurance that what it learns is Truth.

All Truth is Truth. Whatever Truth is revealed in general revelation must therefore be true—not partially so, or even mostly so. To say otherwise is to say that, in nature, God gave us contaminated truth, or no truth at all. Neither can be correct. Revelation from God is always wholly true. But what truth is revealed through general revelation? Is it truth about automobile mechanics? About medicine (think of the changes in that field!)? About cooking? Or biology, or—you name it! Why should psychology be any different? Indeed, there is no proof that psychology—in any of its parts—has been *revealed*.

And, if it were true that general revelation may be found in psychology, we must ask *what* psychology? As has been observed, there are more than 250 differing psychological systems abroad in this country alone, each competing for recognition as the true one. What proliferation! And, who is able in one lifetime to read, understand, and evaluate all of them? There is only one Bible; there are multiple psychologies. Who is to say that any given psychotherapist's system is correct and that it should be imposed upon others? Indeed, to say so in the face of the unparalleled proliferation of theories is arrogance or sheer arrogance. He who affirms this has made himself the standard of truth for everyone else! Yet, if his discoveries were true revelation, he should do that very thing.

Common Grace

There is no question, then, that the psychologist who wants to claim that what he accepts is truth because it has been revealed by God in nature is in a peck of trouble. But, to this is added the notion of "common grace." By that designation, God is supposed to have graciously given truth to all men alike.[7] But is there not a problem there also? Surely, in His grace, God does good to all men; but does He expect all men to be able to understand His book of nature any more than they fail to understand His book of special revelation? Indeed, it is clear that all God revealed about Himself is that He is a good and powerful creator who will hold men responsible (see Romans 1; Psalm 19). He didn't reveal the elements of science—or of psychology. There is nothing in the Bible about revealing psychological truth through general revelation. The Bible looks on general revelation as limited to non-salvific information about the existence of a good creator. And, even this minimal amount of revelation is suppressed by sinful man (Romans 1:18; see also vv. 21–27). Since that is the fact, of what value can psychological theories be? In the eyes of many Christians who are psychologists, "'Natural revelation' [which integrationists fall back on to justify their position] has not supplemented the Bible, but supplanted it in many areas."[8]

Revelation Is from God

Revelation then—all of it, so long as it is information truly revealed by God—is inerrant. Nothing, except that sort of general

---

7   However, there is no support for this notion In common grace, He supplies the rain and the sun to enable all to grow crops for food (Acts 14:17).
8   Isley, *Op. Cit.*, 66.

(nonspecific) revelation of God as the creator of man and things who holds us responsible for knowing that which is found in the "book of nature," can be said to be inerrant. Indeed, it is entirely false to speak of what science discovers as divine *revelation*. It is human *discovery*—and that is all. Revelation comes from God; discovery from man. And the discoveries that are unearthed may or may not be correctly interpreted. Most of the supposed "discoveries" turn out to be nothing more than the views of humans trying to understand nature. Surely, this cannot be rightly termed "revelation."

What is necessary to recognize, then, is that the "facts" unearthed are man's discoveries, not God's revelation. Discoveries come from man at work in his world; revelation comes from God at work in His world. The great difference between revelation and discovery, I repeat, is that the former is always from God; the latter is not.

www.ingramcontent.com/pod-product-compliance
Lightning Source LLC
Chambersburg PA
CBHW070120030426

42335CB00016B/2216

* 9 7 8 1 9 6 0 2 9 7 0 9 9 *